Vincent

van Gogh

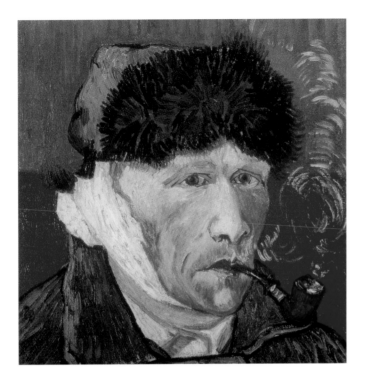

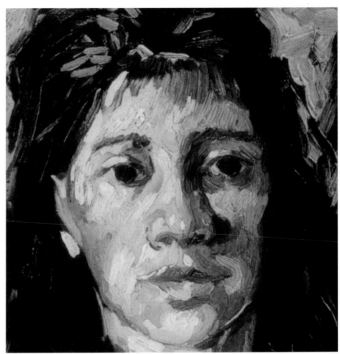

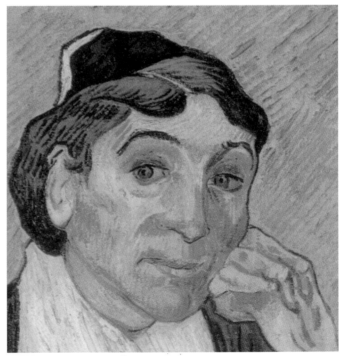

Cover: Stéphanie Angoh
Page layout: Julien Depaulis

© Confidential Concepts, worldwide, USA, 2003
© Sirocco, London, 2003 (English version)

Published in 2003 by Grange Books
an imprint of Grange Books Plc
The Grange Kingsnorth Industrial Estate
Hoo, nr Rochester Kent ME3 9ND
www.Grangebooks.co.uk
ISBN 1-84013-563-8

Vincent

van Gogh

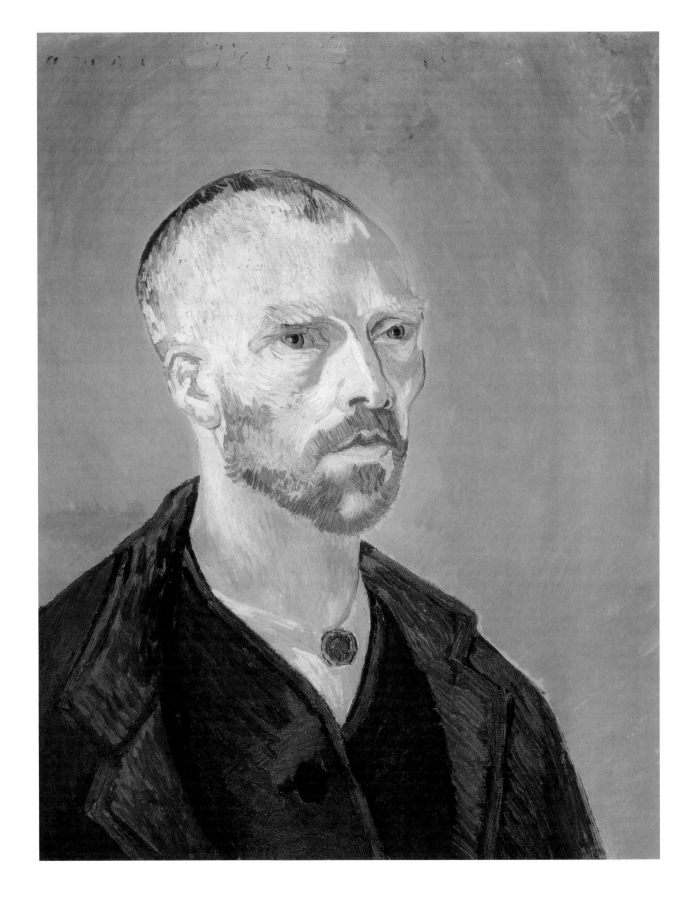

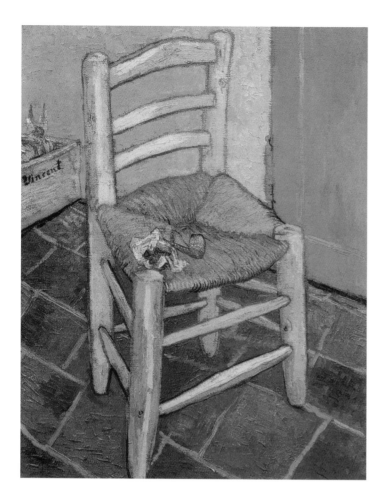

"As through a looking glass, by dark reason…"

V incent Van Gogh's life and work are so intertwined that it is hardly possible to see his pictures without reading in them the story of his life: a life which has been described so many times that it is by now the stuff of legend. Van Gogh is the incarnation of the suffering, misunderstood martyr of modern art, the emblem of the artist as an outsider.

It became apparent early on that the events of Van Gogh's life would play a major role in the reception of his works. The first article about the painter was published in January, 1890 in the *Mercure de France*. The author of the article, Albert Aurier, was in contact with a friend of Van Gogh's named Emile Bernard, from whom he learned the details of Van Gogh's illness. At the time, Van Gogh was living in a mental hospital in Saint-Rémy, near Arles. The year before, he had cut off a piece of his right ear.

1. ***Self-Portrait*** (dedicated to Paul Gauguin), Arles: September 1888. Oil on canvas, 62 x 52 cm. Cambridge, Massachussetts, Fogg Art Museum, Havard University.

2. ***Vincent's Chair with His Pipe***, Arles: December 1888. Oil on canvas, 93 x 73.5 cm. London, National Gallery.

Without explicitly revealing these facts from the artist's life, Aurier nevertheless introduced his knowledge of the apparent insanity of the painter into his discussion of the paintings themselves. Thus, for example, he uses terms like "obsessive passion"[1] and "persistent preoccupation."[2] Van Gogh seems to him a "terrible and demented genius, often sublime, sometimes grotesque, always at the brink of the pathological."[3] Aurier regards the painter as a "Messiah [...] who would regenerate the decrepitude of our art and perhaps of our imbecile and industrialist society."[4]

With this characterization of the artist as a mad genius, the critic lay the foundation for the Van Gogh myth which began to emerge shortly after the death of the painter. After all, Aurier didn't believe that Van Gogh would ever be understood by the general public.

A few days after Van Gogh's funeral in Auvers-sur-Oise, Dr. Gachet, who looked after the painter at the end of his life, wrote to Van Gogh's brother Theo: "This sovereign contempt for life, doubtless a result of his impetuous love of art, is extraordinary. [...] If Vincent were still alive, it would take years and years until the human art triumphed. His death, however, is, so to speak, the glorious result of the fight between two opposed principles: light and darkness, life and death."[5]

In his letters, nearly seven hundred of which have been published, he often writes about his desire for love and safety: "I should like to be with a woman for a change, I cannot live without love, without a woman."[6] Van Gogh's rather bourgeois dreams of hearth and home never finally materialized. His first love, Ursula Loyer, married someone else. His cousin Kee, already a mother and widow, refused him partly for material reasons: Van Gogh was unable to care for her and her child. He tried to build up a family life with a prostitute named Sien. He finally left her because his brother Theo, on whom he depended financially, wanted him to end the relationship. Van Gogh's relationship with the twenty-one-year-old Marguerite Gachet is only known by rumor. Van Gogh not only sought the love of women, but also that of his family and friends, although he never achieved it in the measure he would have wished. Several days before his suicide, he summed up his lifelong failure to find a satisfying intimacy in the following enigmatic remark: "As through a looking glass, by a dark reason – so it has remained."[7] The parson's son had taken his analogy from "The excellencies of love" in the first epistle to the Corinthians: "For now we see through a glass, darkly: but then face to face: now I know in part; but then shall I know even as also I am known."

This longing for a place in the community and the struggle for renown are two themes which can be traced throughout Van Gogh's life.

3. *Vincent's House in Arles* (The Yellow House), Arles : September 1888. Oil on canvas, 72 x 92 cm. Rijksmuseum Vincent van Gogh, Foundation Van Gogh, Amsterdam.

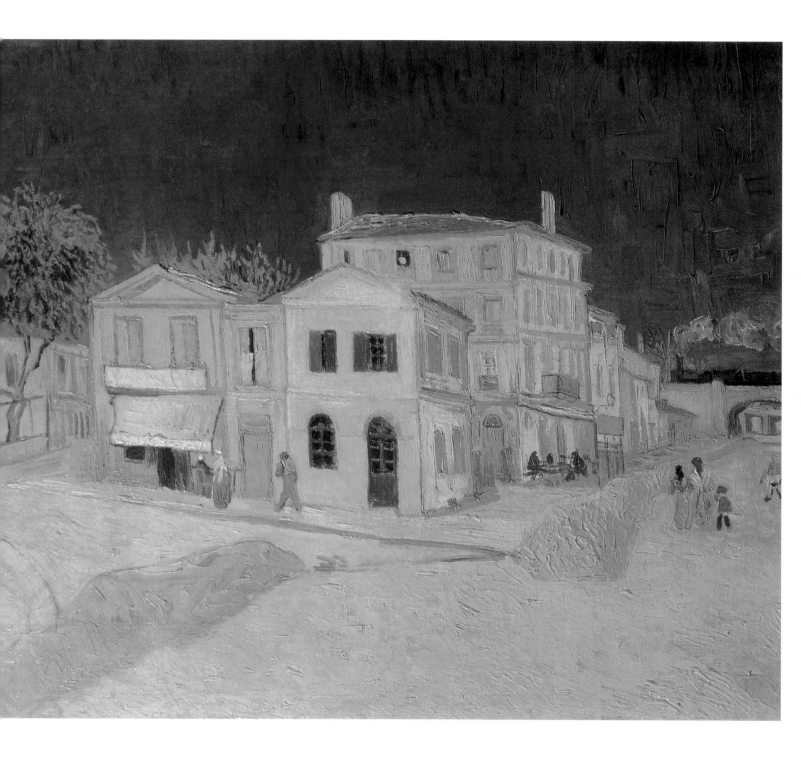

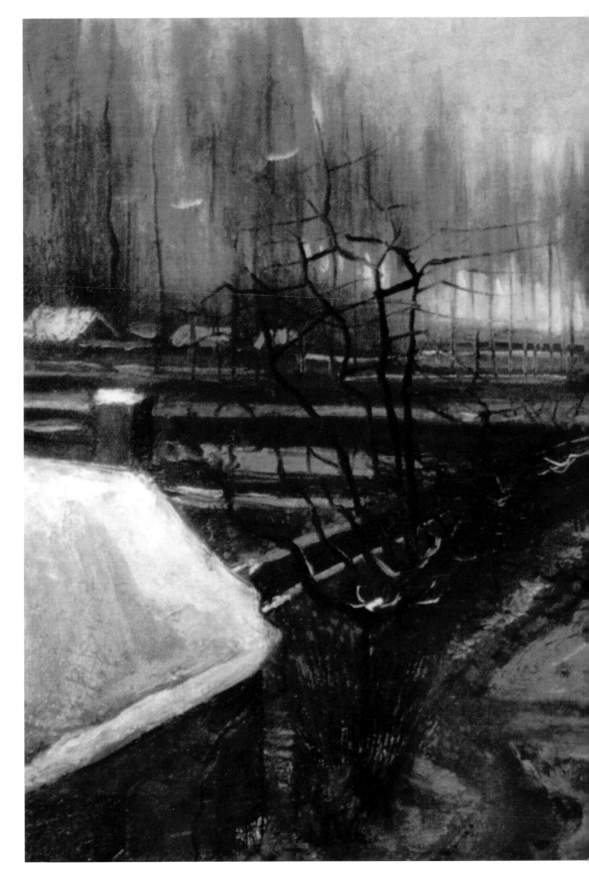

4. *The Parsonage Garden at Nuenen in the Snow*, Nuenen: January 1885. Oil on canvas, 53 x 78 cm. The Armand Hammer Museum of Art.

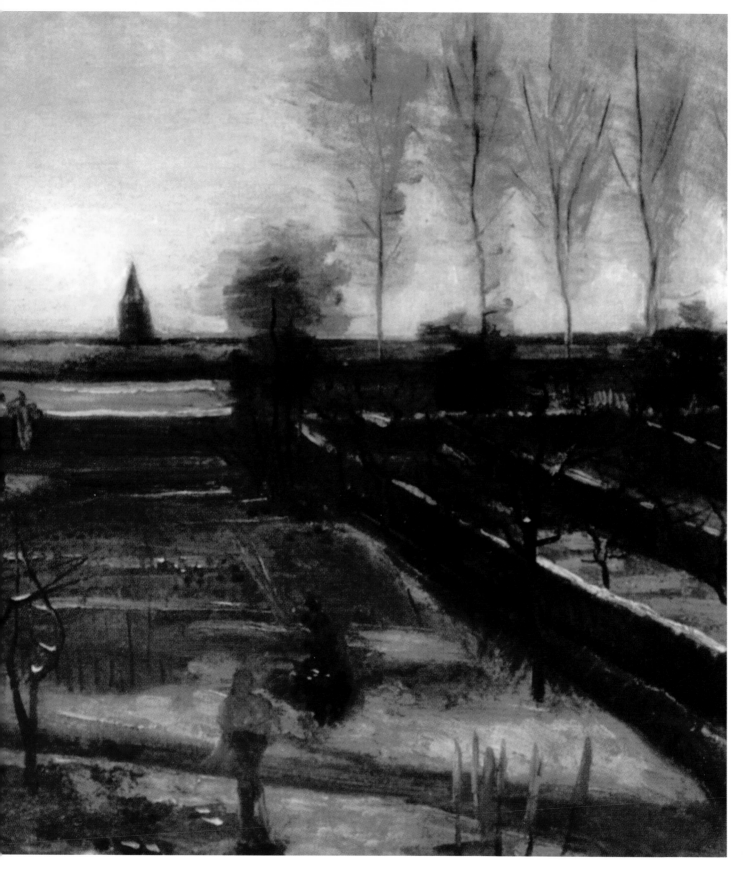

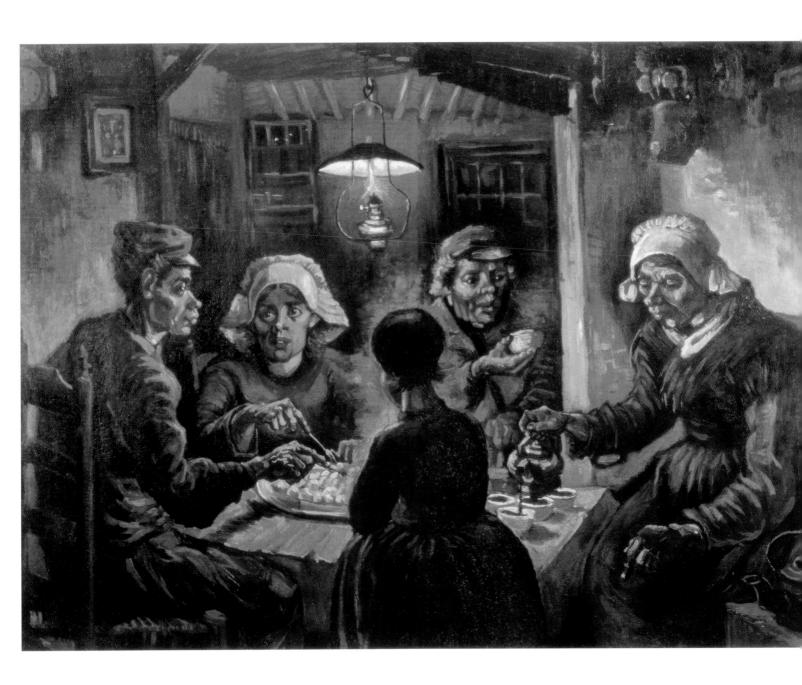

"Feeling nowhere so much myself a stranger as in my family and country... "
Holland, England and Belgium, 1853-1886

"On March 30th, 1852, a dead son was born at the vicarage of Zundert, but a year later on the same date Anna van Gogh gave birth to a healthy boy." [8] Pastor Theodorus van Gogh gave his second born son the same name as the first: Vincent. When the second Vincent walked to his father's church to attend services, he passed by the grave where 'his' name was written on a tombstone. In the last months of his life, Van Gogh reminisced about the places of his childhood, and often wistfully mentioned the graveyard of Zundert.

Very little is known about Van Gogh as a child. A neighbor's daughter described him as "kind-hearted, friendly, good, pitiful," [9] while a former servant girl of the family reported that "Vincent had 'oarige' (funny, meaning unpleasantly eccentric) manners." [10]

Similar inconsistencies appear in descriptions of Van Gogh as an adult. In general, Van Gogh was kind and compassionate toward the poor or sick, and also to children. Another important trait that emerged early on, according to the artist's sister Elisabeth Huberta, was his close relation to nature: "He knew the places where the rarest flowers bloomed [...] as regards birds, he knew exactly where each nested or lived, and if he saw a pair of larks descend in the rye field, he knew how to approach their nest without snapping the surrounding blades or harming the birds in the least." [11]

In his last years, Van Gogh returned to the landscapes of his childhood through painting. "The whole south, everything became Holland for him," [12] said Paul Gauguin of the paintings Van Gogh made in Arles. In a letter to Emile Bernard, Van Gogh compared the heath and flat landscape of the Carmargue with Holland. While staying in the mental hospital of Saint-Rémy he wrote to Theo: "During my illness I saw again every room in the house at Zundert, every path, every plant in the garden, the views of the fields outside, the neighbors, the graveyard, the church, our kitchen garden at the back – down to a magpie's nest in a tall acacia in the graveyard." [13]

The references to nests made by both Elisabeth Huberta and by Van Gogh himself suggests the extent of the importance of this image for the painter. The nest is a symbol of safety, which may explain why he called houses "human nests." [14]

Van Gogh had to leave his first nest – his parents' home – at the age of eleven. It is not clear why the elder Van Gogh decided to send his son to a boarding school in Zevenbergen, some thirty kilometers from Zundert.

5. ***The Potato Eaters***,
Nuenen, April 1885,
Oil on canvas,
81.5 x 114.5 cm,
Foundation Van Gogh,
Amsterdam.

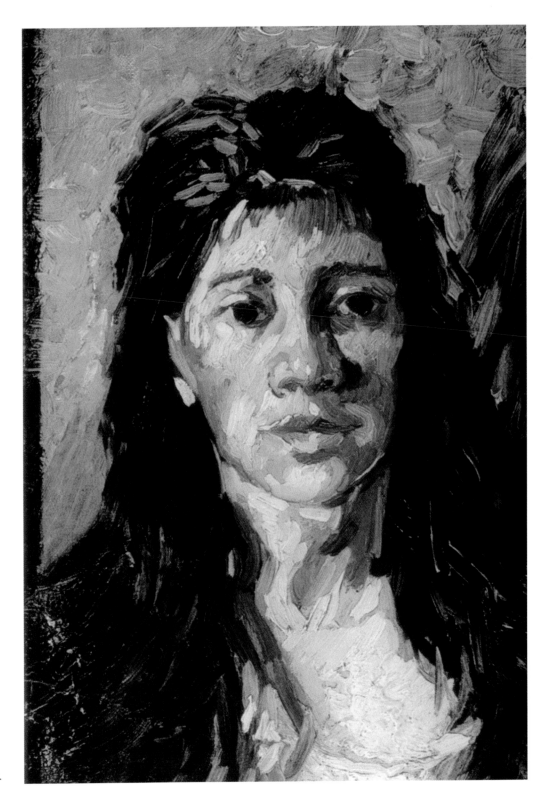

6. *Portrait of a Woman
   in Blue*, Antwerp,
   December 1885.
   Oil on canvas,
   46 x 38.5 cm.
   Rijksmuseum Vincent
   van Gogh, Foundation
   Van Gogh, Amsterdam.

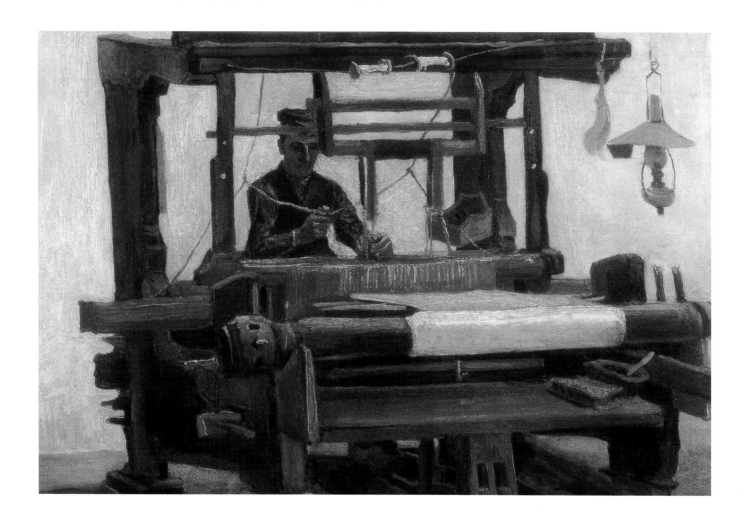

Perhaps there was no Protestant school nearby; the neighborhood of Zundert was almost entirely Catholic. Or perhaps the parents' nest had simply become too small with the arrival of four more children. A few weeks before his death, Van Gogh painted his memory of this farewell: a two-wheel carriage rolling through fields on a narrow path. At the age of thirteen, Vincent went to a higher school in Tilburg, where the landscape painter Constantijn C. Huysmans taught him drawing. During his stay in Tilburg the first of two known photographs of young Van Gogh was taken. It shows a soft, boyish face with very light eyes. The second portrait shows Van Gogh as an earnest 19 year old. By then, he had already been at work for three years in The Hague, at the gallery of Goupil & Co, where one of Van Gogh's uncles was a partner. Van Gogh's master at Goupil's was the 24-year-old Hermanus Gijsbertus Tersteeg. Later, when Van Gogh had begun his career as a painter, he would continue struggling – always in vain – to win the respect of the highly regarded dealer.

7. *Weaver, Seen from the Front*, Neunen, May 1884.
Oil on canvas, 70 x 85 cm.
Otterlo, Rijksmuseum Kröller-Müller.

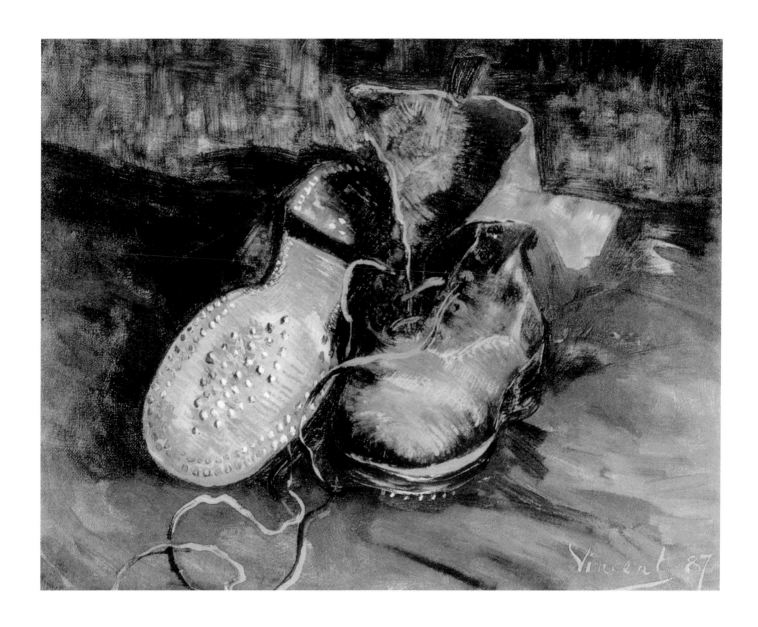

8. *Pair of Shoes*, Paris,
   early 1887. Oil on
   canvas, 34 x 41.5 cm,
   Baltimore, The
   Baltimore Museum of
   Art, The Cone
   Collection.

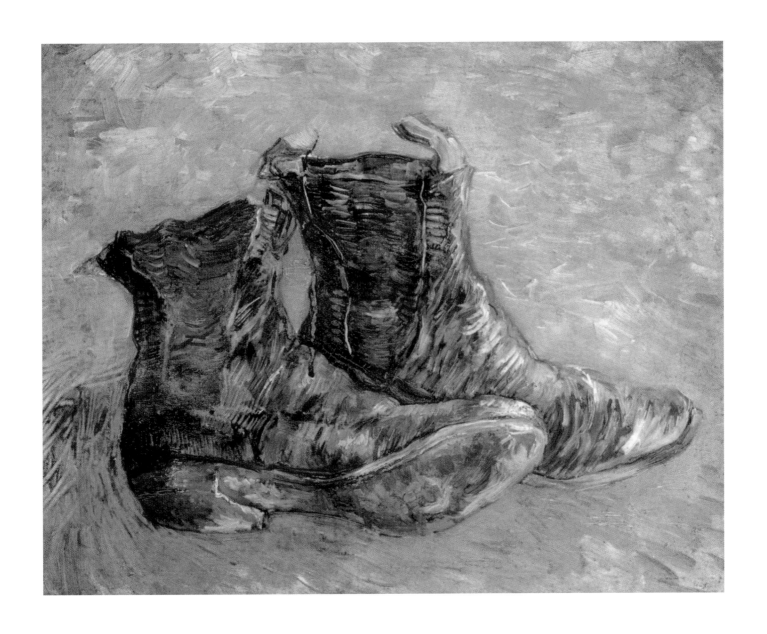

9. *Pair of Shoes*, Paris,
   Spring 1887;
   Oil on cardboard,
   33 x 41 cm.
   Rijksmuseum Vincent
   van Gogh, Foundation
   Van Gogh, Amsterdam.

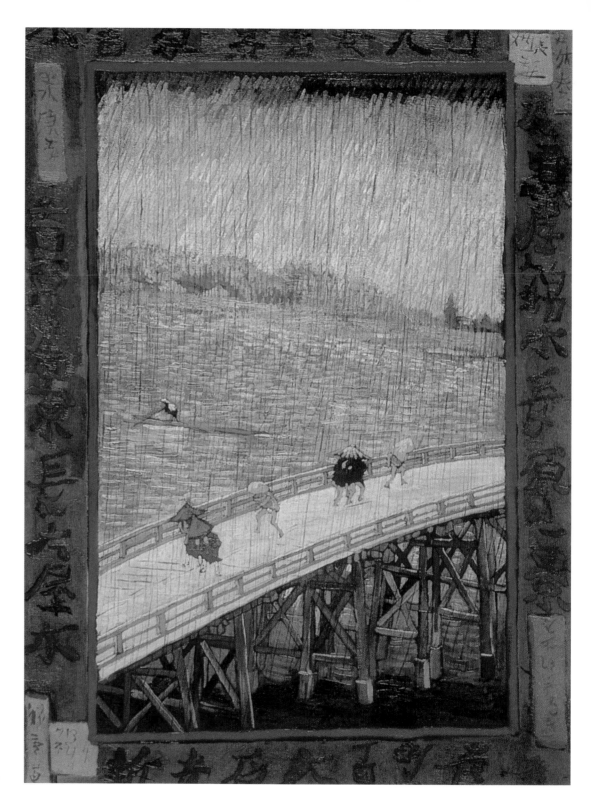

10. *Japonaiserie : Bridge in the Rain* (*after Hiroshige*), Paris, September-October 1887. Oil on canvas, 73 x 54 cm. Rijksmuseum Vincent van Gogh, Foundation Van Gogh, Amsterdam.

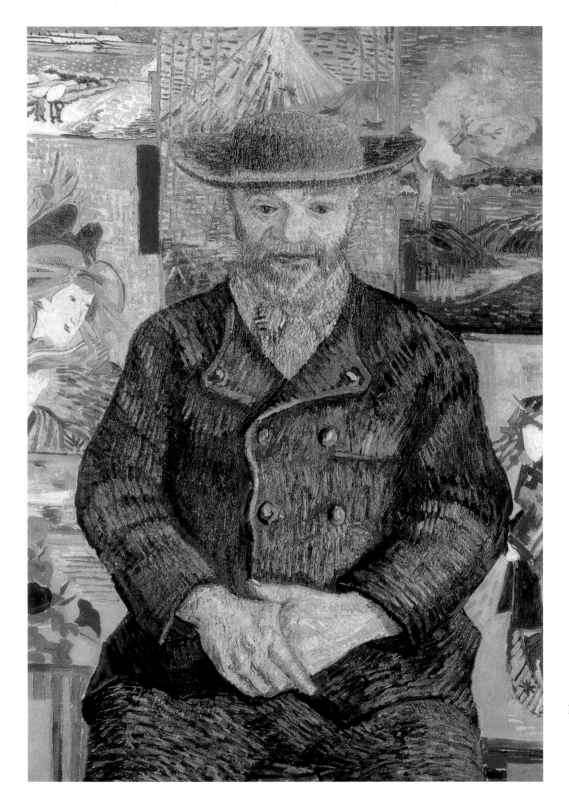

11. *Portrait of Père Tanguy*, Paris, Automn 1887. Oil on canvas, 92 x 75 cm. Paris, Musée Rodin.

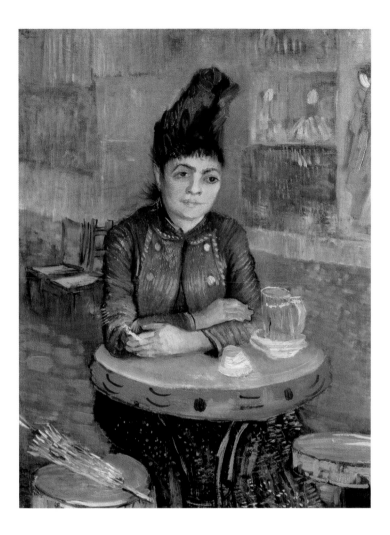

12. **Agostina Segatori Sitting in the Cafe Tambourin**, Paris, February-March 1887. Oil on canvas, 55.5 x 46.5 cm, Rijksmuseum Vincent van Gogh, Foundation Van Gogh, Amsterdam.

13. **Le Moulin de la Galette**, Paris, March 1887. Oil on canvas, 46 x 38 cm. Pittsburgh, Museum of Art, Carnegie Institute.

During his apprenticeship, Van Gogh came into contact with the paintings of the salons and of the school of Barbizon, whose most distinguished representative, Jean-François Millet (1814 – 1875), became one of the most influential figures for the painter. As Goupil & Co. also sold prints, the trainee saw reproductions of many masterpieces. Here, Van Gogh built his new nest: the gallery, and later the museums, became his "land of pictures." [15]

In August 1872, Theo came to see his elder brother in The Hague. During this meeting the two young men, then 19 and 15 years old, became closer in a way that changes relatives into friends. Thereafter, Vincent regarded Theo as his alter ego. Vincent wrote more than 600 letters in 18 years to his brother, who collected them faithfully. Most of these were published after Van Gogh's death. Roughly 40 of Theo's letters survived.

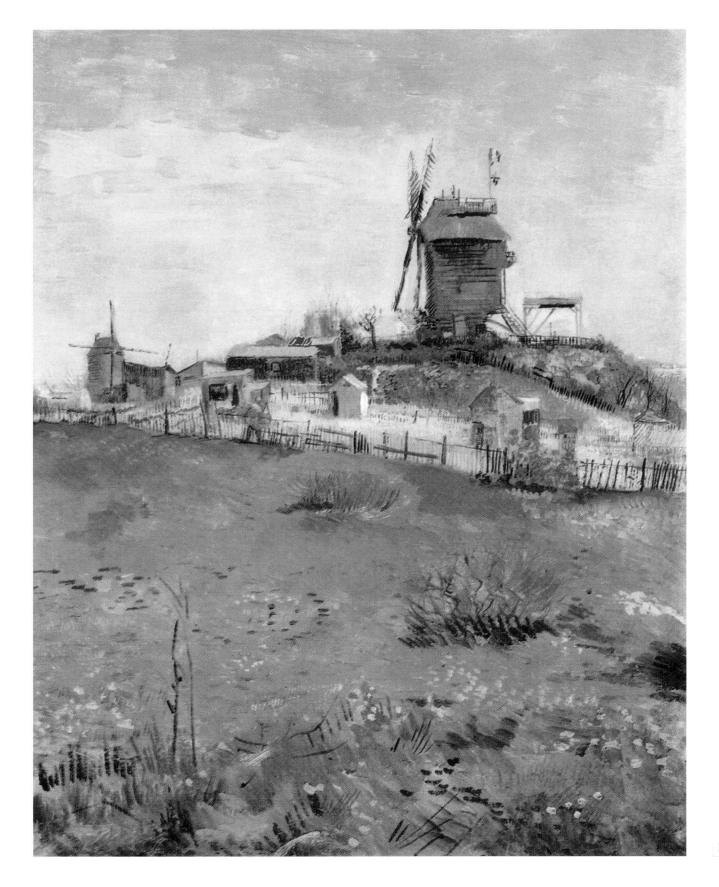

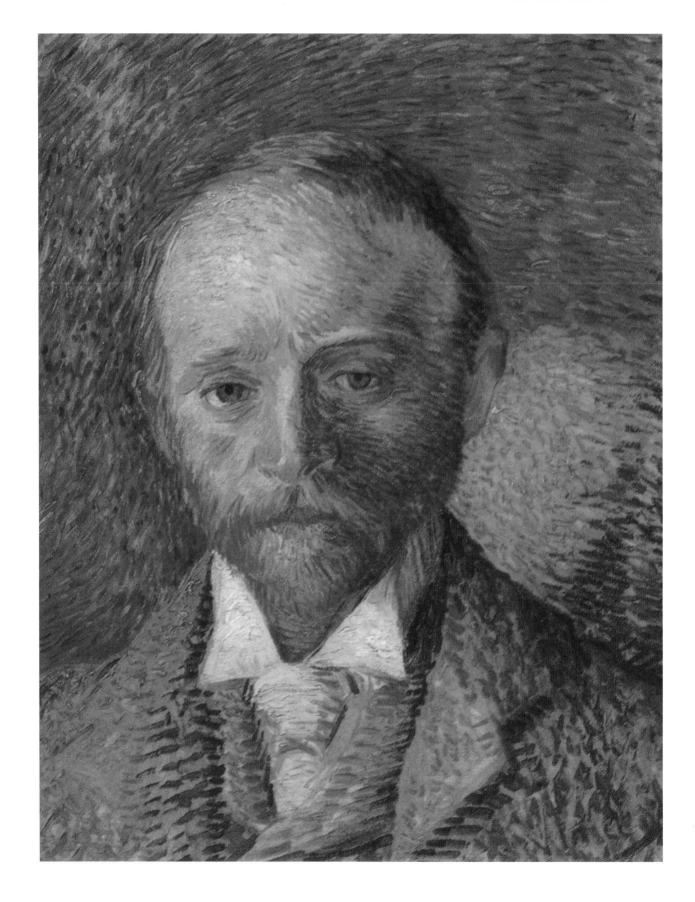

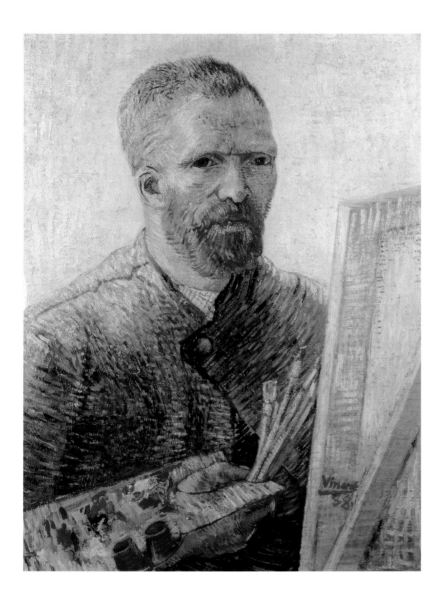

The others were the casualties of Vincent's frequent relocations, in which a large number of drawings and painting were also lost. Van Gogh recalled wistfully in the summer of 1873. By then his training had come to an end, and the young man found himself working for Goupil's in London. Ten years later, just as he was about to become an artist, he remembered: "In London how often I stood drawing on the Thames Embankment, on my way home from Southampton Street in the evening, and it came to nothing." [16] His favorite reading in London was *L'amour* by Jules Michelet: "To me the book has been both a revelation and a Gospel at the same time [...] And that man and wife can be one, that is to say, one whole and not two halves, yes, I believe that too." [17]

14. ***Portrait of the Art Dealer Alexandre Reid***, Paris, Spring 1887, Oil on canvas, 41.5 x 33.5 cm, Glasgow, Glasgow Art Gallery and Museum.

15. ***Self-Portrait in Front of the Easel***, Paris, January-February 1888, Oil on canvas, 65 x 50.5 cm, Rijksmuseum Vincent van Gogh, Foundation Van Gogh, Amsterdam.

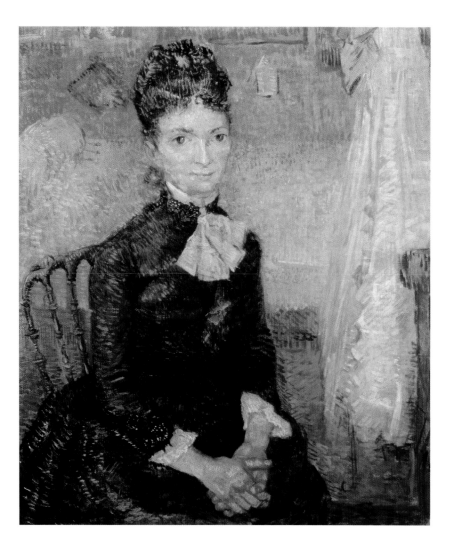

16. **Woman Sitting by a Cradle**, Paris, Spring 1887. Oil on canvas, 61 x 46 cm. Rijksmuseum Vincent van Gogh, Foundation Van Gogh, Amsterdam.

17. **Portrait of Armand Roulin**, Arles, Nov-Dec 1888. Oil on canvas, 65 x 54 cm, Rotterdam, Museum Boymans-van Beuningen.

When Van Gogh wrote these sentences at the end of July, 1874, he had every hope that his revelation would be fulfilled. But his love for Ursula Loyer, the daughter of his landlady, ended in disaster. She was already engaged when Van Gogh met her, and it was not his decision to leave London; in May, 1875, he was transferred to Paris – against his will.

By this time, Van Gogh had already given up his Gospel of earthly love and turned instead to the love of God. His religious enthusiasm was perhaps one reason why he had to leave Goupil's in London. The business, moved into a bigger house, was no longer just a stockroom but a public gallery. And the solitary and eccentric Van Gogh had difficulty pleasing the clientele. His family may also have wanted to bring an end to his "affair" with Ursula.

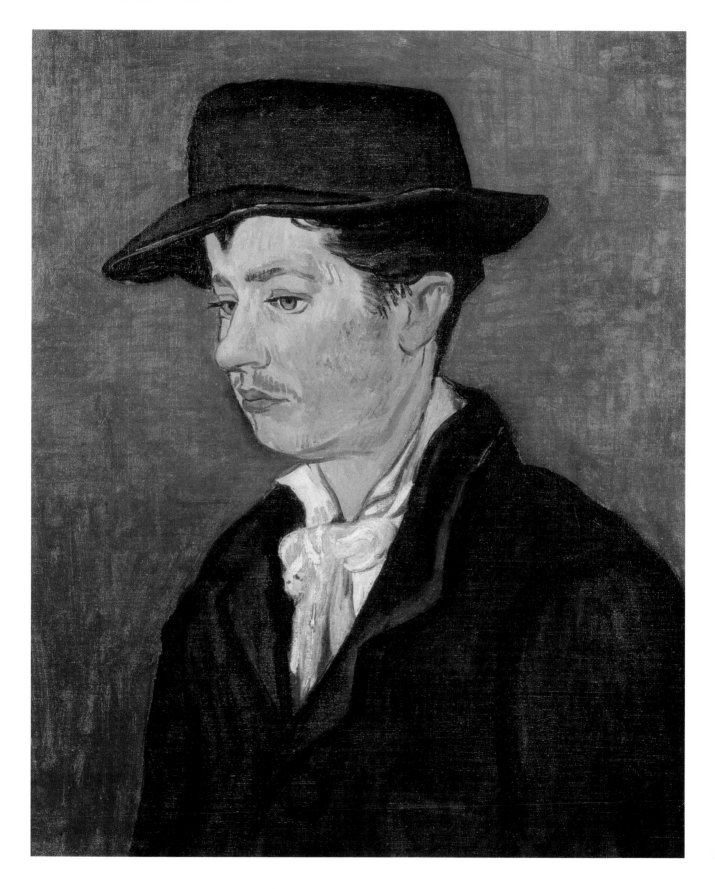

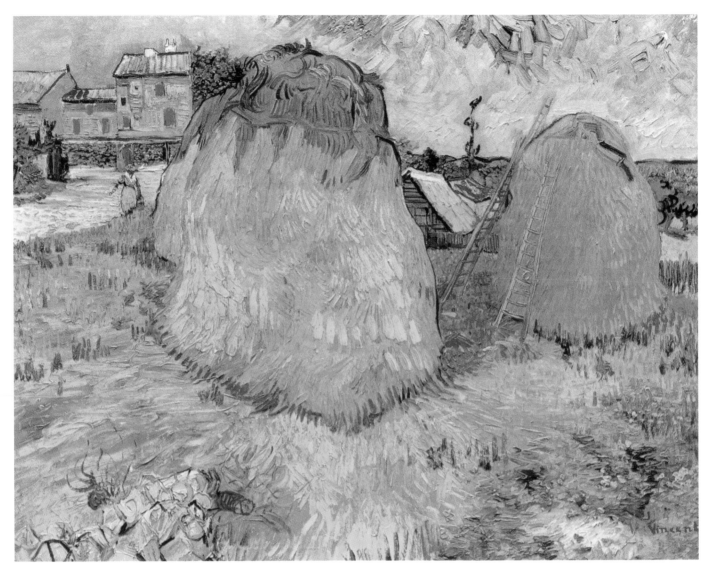

18. ***Haystacks in Provence***, Arles, June 1888. Oil on canvas, 73 x 92.5 cm. Otterlo, Rijksmuseum Kröller-Müller.

19. ***Still Life: Vase with Fifteen Sunflowers***, Arles, August 1888. Oil on canvas, 93 x 73 cm. London, National Gallery.

Van Gogh himself suspected his father and uncle of being behind the transfer. He retaliated with silence – a weapon that he came to rely on quite often in conflicts. Theo, who had taken Vincent's place in Goupil's office in The Hague, thus became the only member of the family with whom Van Gogh maintained contact. The brothers continued to exchange their opinions about art. Vincent wrote often of his visits to the Louvre, and in particular, of his passion for the paintings of Ruysdael and Rembrandt. Above all else, Van Gogh was an enthusiast, not a dealer, and he had little patience for the paintings he was supposed to sell at Goupil's.

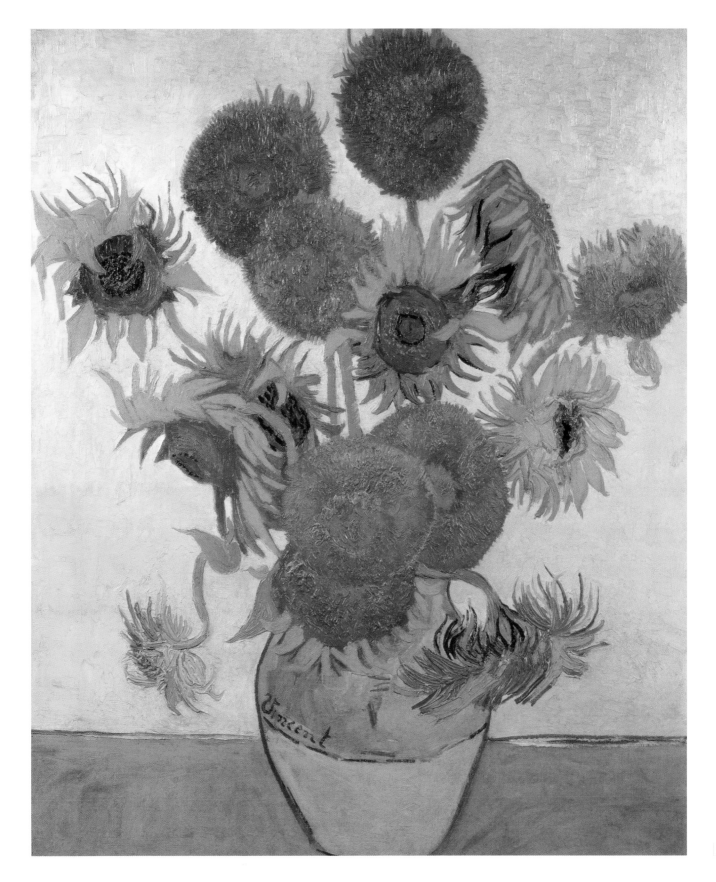

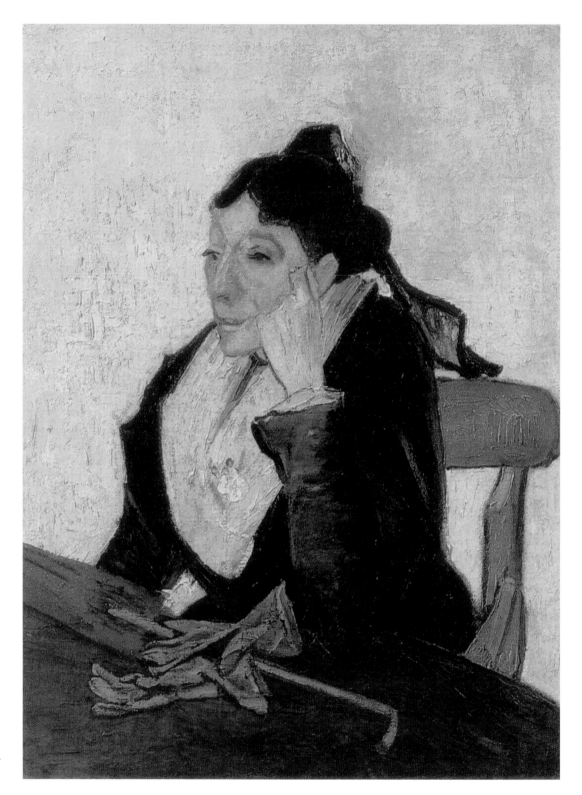

20. *L'Arlésienne :*
    Madame Ginoux wtih
    Gloves and an
    Umbrella, Arles, early
    November 1888, Oil
    on canvas, 93 x 74 cm,
    Paris, Musée d'Orsay.

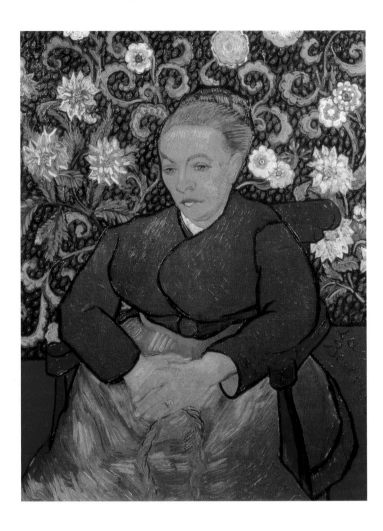

His parents were informed of his failure in the business. When Vincent came home for Christmas in 1875 – clearly without having obtained permission to leave the gallery during the busiest time of the year – his father suggested that he resign. But by then it was already too late, and the gallery manager dismissed Van Gogh immediately after his return to Paris.

Van Gogh decided not to return to Holland, but to England. He found work as an assistant teacher in Ramsgate, and later as an assistant preacher in Isleworth. When he returned to Holland to join his family for Christmas, his parents had already decided to change the direction of his journey through life, by steering him into the bookstore of Pieter Kornelius Braat in Dordrecht. Vincent accepted and took a position in the accounting department of the shop. But his Bible studies continued to be his main interest.

21. *Madam Roulin Rocking the Cradle*, *La Berceuse*, Arles, January 1889. Oil on canvas, 92 x 73 cm. Otterlo, Rijksmuseum Kröller-Müller.

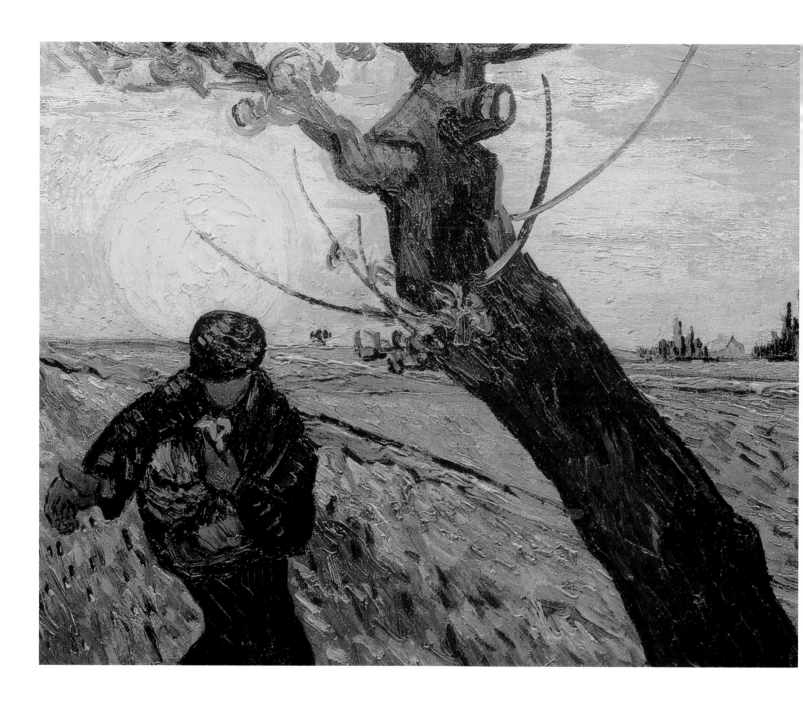

On his first Sunday in Dordrecht, Van Gogh went to church twice to listen to a sermon about this verse from the first epistle to the Corinthians: "Now we look through a mirror into a dark reason, now I only know in part, but then I shall know even as also I am known myself." [18] Van Gogh's understanding of the biblical verse reveals his yearning to be known. This desire persisted through most of his life, manifesting itself in his friendship with Theo, in his love for Ursula Loyer or his cousin Kee, and in his attitudes about religion or art. The common thread in each of these is an intense longing to discover himself in a dialogue with others. The mercantile affairs of an art dealer or an accountant offered no such satisfaction. During his stay in Dordrecht, Van Gogh finally arrived at a plan for his future: he set out to become a minister.

P. C. Görlitz, Van Gogh's roommate in this time, wrote of him: "He was totally different from the usual type of man. His face was ugly, his mouth more or less awry, his face was densely covered with freckles, and he had hair of a reddish hue. As I said, his face was ugly, but as soon as he spoke about religion or art, and then became excited, which was sure to happen very soon, his eyes would sparkle, and his features would make a deep impression on me; it wasn't his own face any longer: it had become beautiful [...] When he came back from his office at nine o'clock in the evening, he would immediately light a little wooden pipe; he would take down a big Bible, and sit down to read assiduously, to copy texts and to learn them by heart; he would also write all kinds of religious compositions [...] When Sunday came Van Gogh would go to church three times, either to the Roman Catholic church, or to the Protestant or Old Episcopal church, which was commonly called the Jansenist church. When once we made the remark, "But, my dear Van Gogh, how is it possible that you can go to three churches of such divergent creeds?" he said, "Well, in every church I see God, and it's all the same to me whether a Protestant pastor or a Roman Catholic priest preaches; it is not really a matter of dogma, but of the spirit of the Gospel, and I find this spirit in all churches." [19]

After his failure as a businessman, Van Gogh hoped that his father would appreciate his decision to follow in his footsteps. But vicar Van Gogh viewed his eldest son's enthusiasm for religion critically: Vincent's belief in the "spirit of the Gospel" deviated from the teachings of the Church. In May, 1977 Van Gogh began to prepare himself for the university. Van Gogh stayed less than one year in Amsterdam, and then he abandoned his studies. He did not lack talent – Van Gogh spoke a couple of languages, read German books, and wrote his letters in English and French.

22. *The Sower*, Arles,
November 1888.
Oil on canvas,
32 x 40 cm.
Rijksmuseum Vincent
van Gogh, Foundation
Van Gogh, Amsterdam.

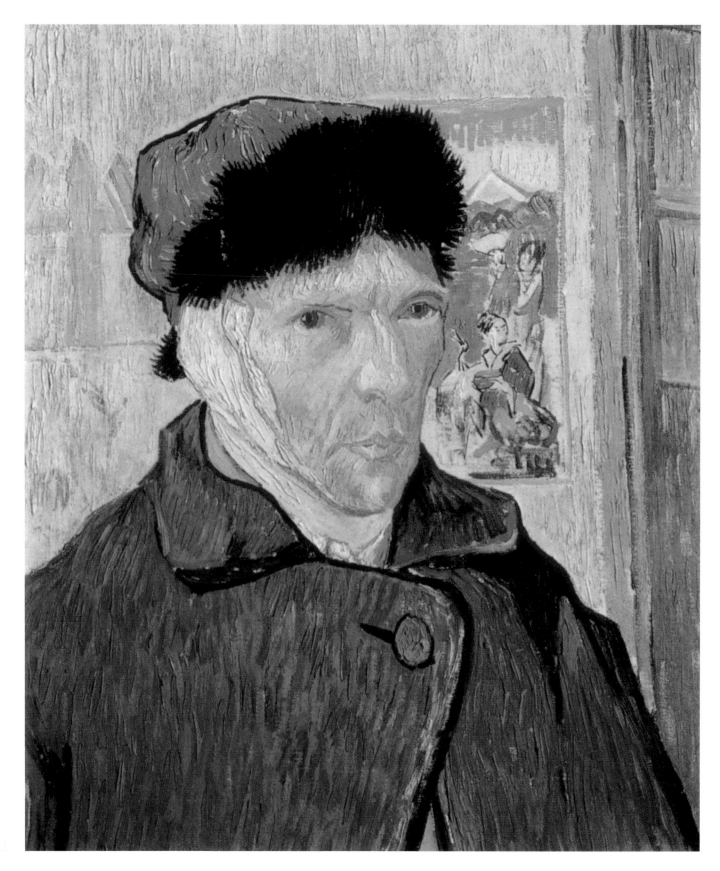

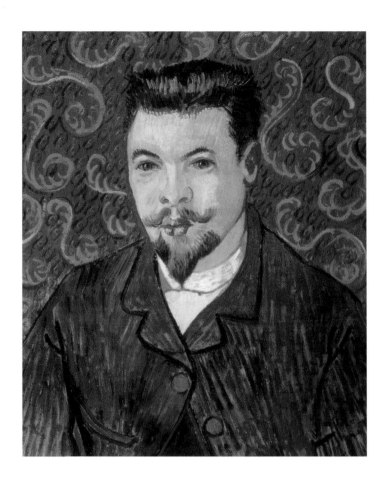

But he was impatient; he did not want to meditate on the Gospel; he wanted to live it. He travelled to Brussels to begin training at a mission school. Three months later, he left the school and applied for a job as a preacher in the Borinage, a Belgian mining area. In January, 1879, he found a temporary post that might have been renewed if an inspector of the Comité d'Evangélisation had not discovered that the new preacher took the Bible more literally than the authorities of the church. After he 'failed' as preacher, Van Gogh broke with the church, which was, in his opinion, dominated by Christian conventions instead of a Christ-like love for mankind. This rupture also sent ripples through his relationship with his father, who threatened to have his son committed to the mental hospital in Gheel. [20]

After his father's death in 1885, Van Gogh expressed his resentment against father and church in two still lifes: one shows his father's pipe and tobacco pouch lying next to a vase with a bouquet of flowers, known in Holland as silver of Judas.

23. *Self-Portrait With Bandaged Ear*, Arles, January 1889. Oil on canvas, 60 x 49 cm. London, Courtauld Institute.

24. *Portrait of Doctor Félix Rey*, Arles, January 1889. Oil on canvas, 64 x 53 cm. Moscow, Pouchkin Museum.

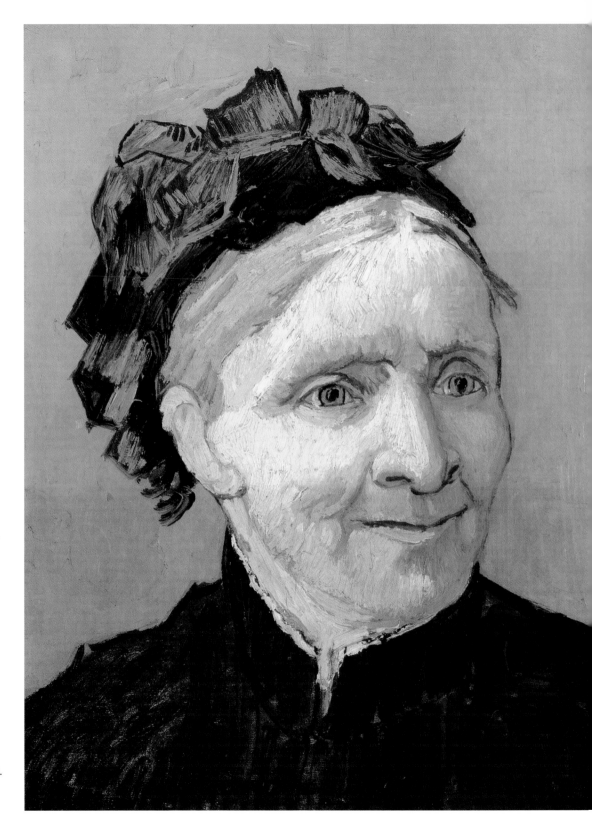

25. ***Portrait of the Artist's Mother***, Arles, October 1888, Oil on canvas, 40.5 x 32.5 cm, Pasadena, California, Norton Simon Museum of Art.

26. ***The Zouave*** (half length), Arles, June 1888. Oil on canvas, 65 x 54 cm, Rijksmuseum Vincent van Gogh, Foundation Van Gogh, Amsterdam.

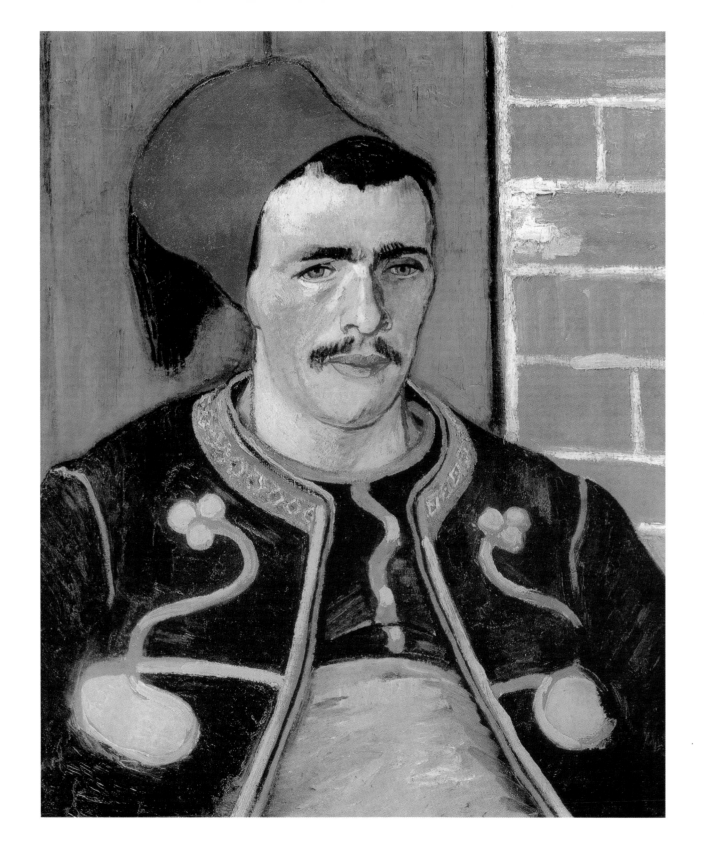

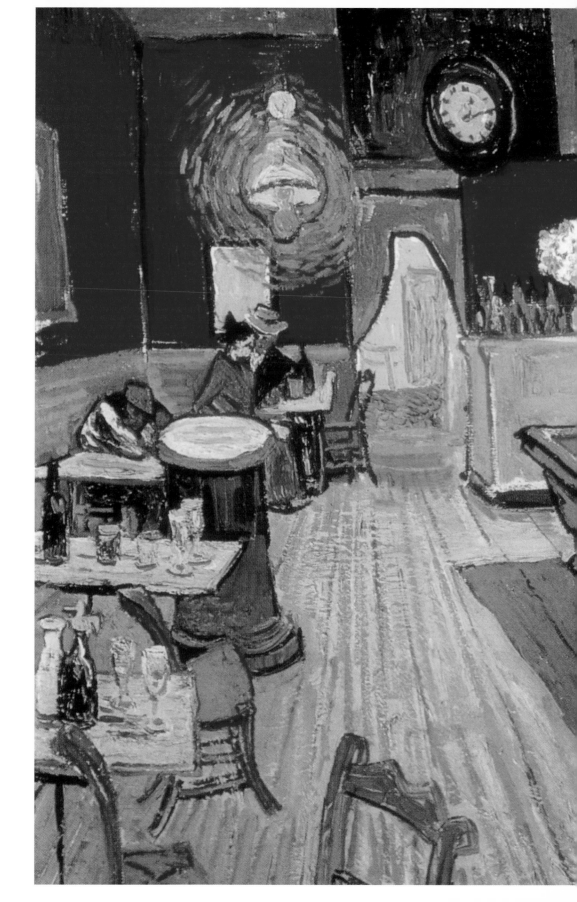

27. *Café at Night*, Arles,
September 1888.
Watercolor,
44 x 63 cm. Berne,
Private Collection.

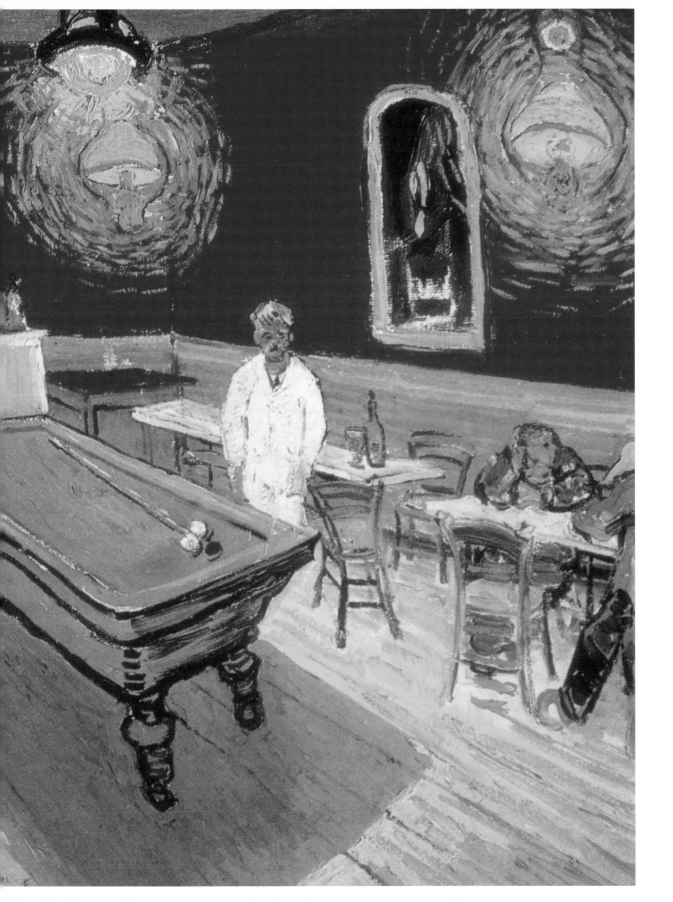

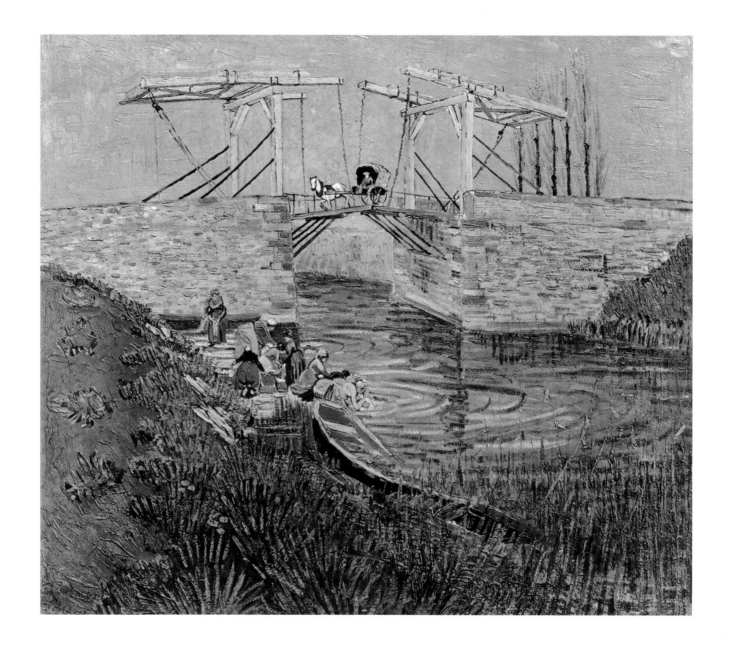

28. *Langlois Bridge at
Arles*. Arles, April
1888. Oil on canvas,
60 x 65 cm, Paris.
Private Collection.

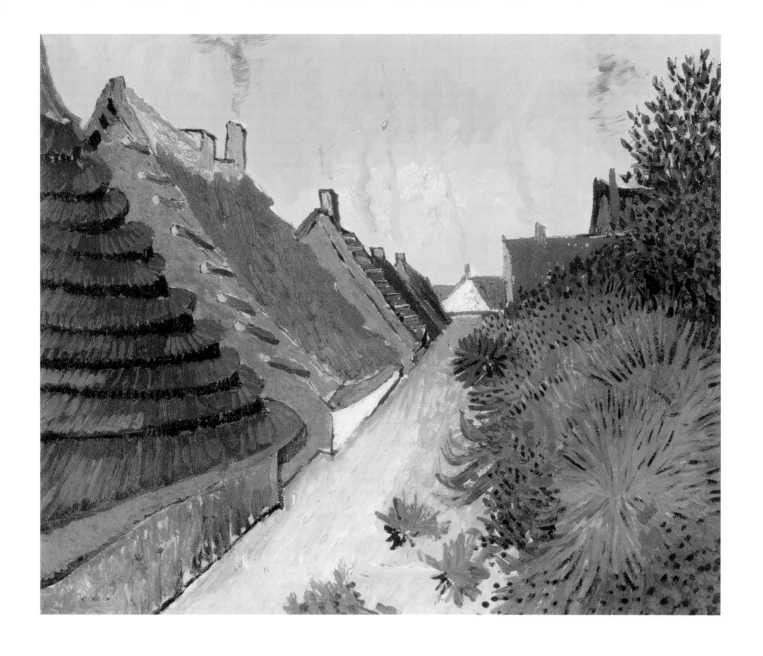

29. ***Street in Saintes-
Maries***, Arles, early
June 1888.
Oil on canvas,
38 x 46.1 cm,
Private Collection.

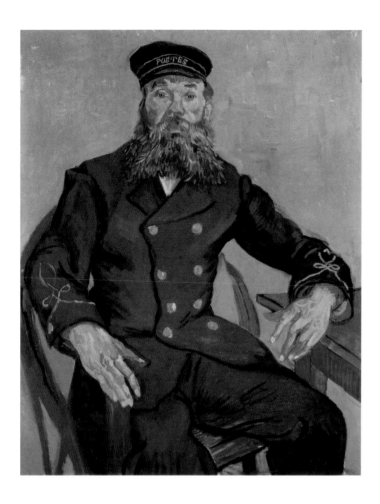

The second composition depicts a large, open Bible next to a small, well-thumbed copy of Zola's *Joie de vivre* – "The joy of life". Vicar Van Gogh disapproved of his son's preference for contemporary French literature, which was – in his opinion – depraved. The correspondence between autumn 1879 and spring 1880 is full of gaps. Van Gogh remained in the Borinage, where he spent most of his time drawing. He had already started to make sketches in Brussels and during his time as a preacher: "Often I draw far into the night, to keep some souvenir and to strengthen the thoughts raised involuntarily by the aspect of things here." [21]

The 'renewed' Van Gogh made two important decisions: First, he resolved to determine the course of his life entirely on his own and not to seek his family's advice; second, he set out to put his passions to good use: "When I was in other surroundings, in the surroundings of pictures and works of art, you know how violent a passion I had for them, reaching the highest pitch of enthusiasm.

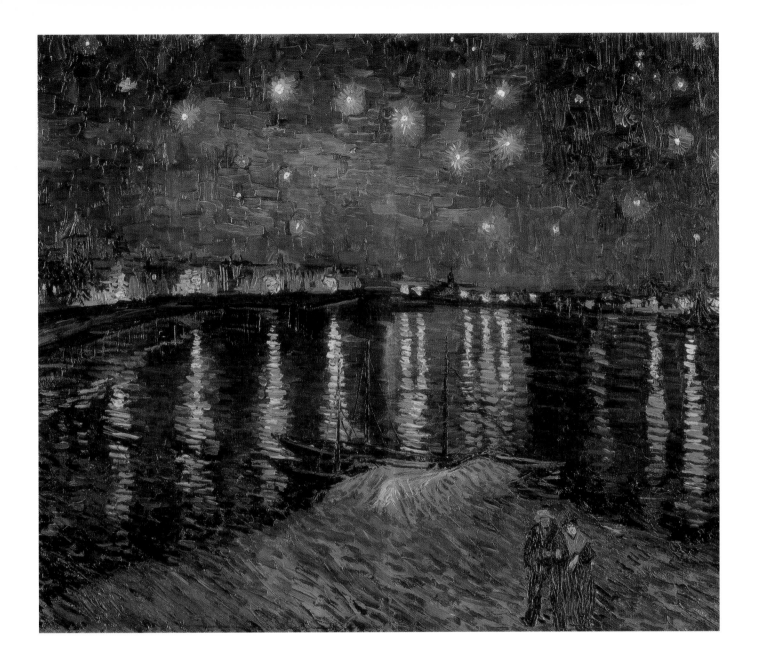

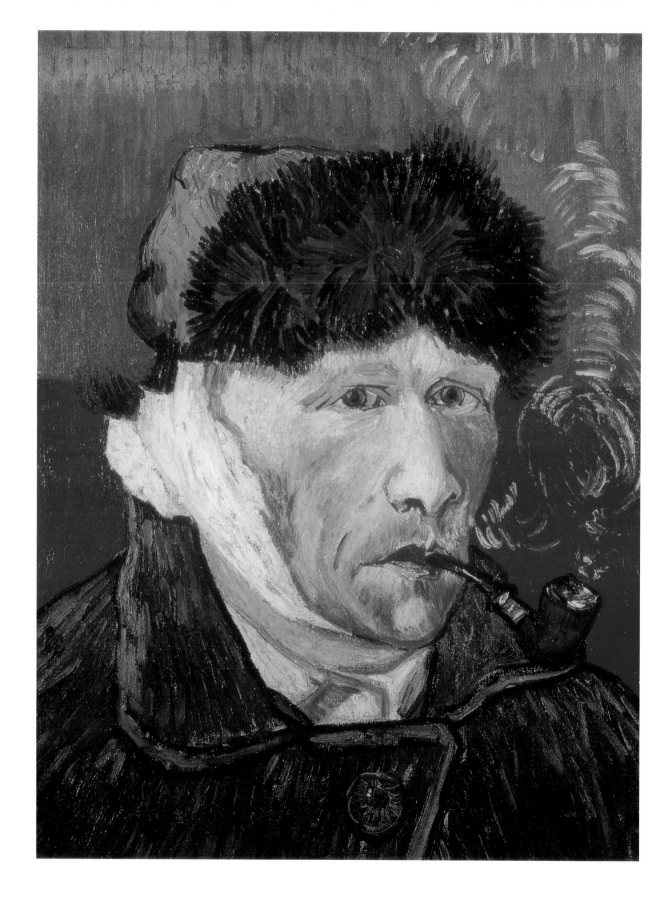

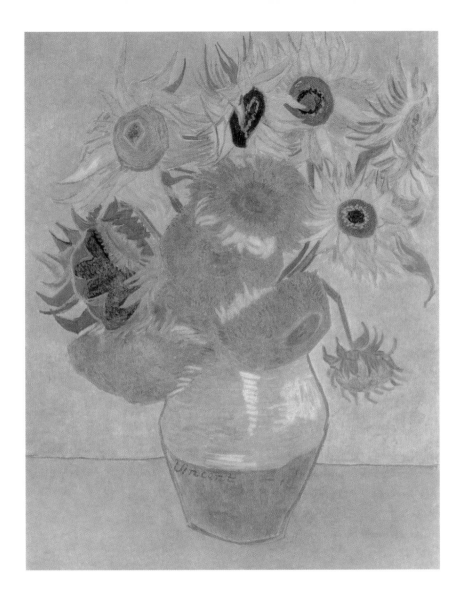

And I am not sorry about it, for even now, far from that land, I am often homesick for the land of pictures." [22] Homesick for the world of art, Van Gogh moved to Brussels in October, 1880. He began to study with reproductions and models. Though his father disapproved of his decision, he supported his son financially. Theo, who by that time had begun working in Goupil's branch in Paris, also sent him money. In the spring of 1881, to reduce his expenses, Van Gogh moved to the vicarage in Etten, where his father had been working for some time. The young painter did not suffer from material wants, but his family neither understood nor supported his ideas: "Father and Mother are very good to me in that they do everything to feed me well, etc.

32. *Self-Portrait with Bandaged Ear and Pipe*, Arles, January 1889. Oil on canvas, 51 x 45 cm. Private Collection, Chicago

33. *Still-life: Vase with Twelve Sunflowers*, Arles, January 1889. Oil on canvas, 92 x 72.5 cm. Philadelphia, The Philadelphia Museum of Art.

Of course I appreciate it very much, but it cannot be denied that food and drink and sleep are not enough for a man, that he longs for something nobler and higher – aye, he positively cannot do without it."[23] At this time, "something nobler and higher" meant, first of all, not the artistic work, but his love for his cousin Kee. Although she had resisted his advances, he continued trying to win her heart. His family was ashamed by his persistence, and openly criticized his passion. After a particularly heated argument during the Christmas holidays in 1881, the pastor ordered his wayward son to leave.

Two years later Vincent returned to the family nest for the last time. With this final break, he abandoned the family name, and began signing his canvases simply 'Vincent.' The event which precipitated the rupture was Van Gogh's decision to take up residence in The Hague with the prostitute Christina Hoornik, called Sien. The compassion he felt for the pregnant woman was coupled with his longing to have a nest: "I have a feeling of being at home when I am with her, as though she gives me my own hearth, a feeling that our lives are interwoven."[24]

The family reacted with reproaches, exhortations, and threats. For some time Van Gogh had been dependent on people who did not accept him, a paradox which prompted him to think at length about the relationship between art and money. He wrote to Theo: "I will succeed in earning money to keep myself, not in luxury, but as one who eats his bread in the sweat of his brow."[25] In the years to come, Van Gogh would defend the artist as a productive – and therefore respectable – member of society. He began sending Theo some of his pictures in exchange for the money he sent; in this way Theo became his employer rather than his patron.

In The Hague, Van Gogh focused on figurative drawing. Sien was his most important model: "I find in her exactly what I want: her life has been rough, and sorrow and adversity have put their marks upon her – now I can do something with her."[26] Van Gogh's conception of women was quite far removed from the classical ideal of beauty. On one occasion, he expressed his opinion in these terms: "For what's the use of a beautiful body? Animals have it too, perhaps even more than men; but the soul, as it lives in the people painted by Israëls or Millet or Frère, that is what animals never have. Is not life given to us to become richer in spirit, even though the outward appearance may suffer?"[27] For some time Van Gogh served as an apprentice to the painter Anton Mauve. There, he started to paint with oil colors. His major motifs involved people: "I am decidedly not a landscape painter; when I make landscapes, there will always be something of the figure in them."[28] When Mauve discovered that Van Gogh was living together with Sien, he canceled the contact.

34. *Ward in the Hospital in Arles*, April 1889, Oil on canvas, 74 x 92 cm, Winterthur, Collection Oskar Reinhart.

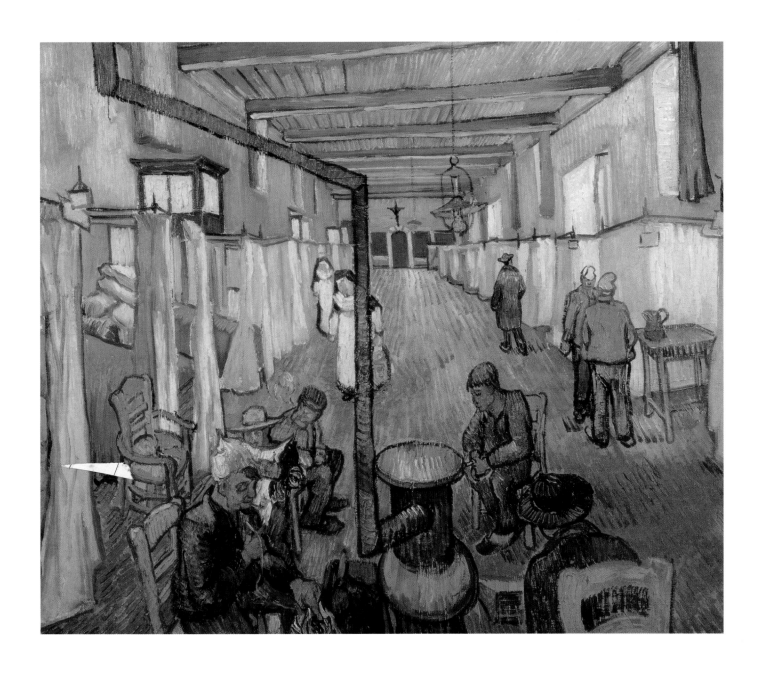

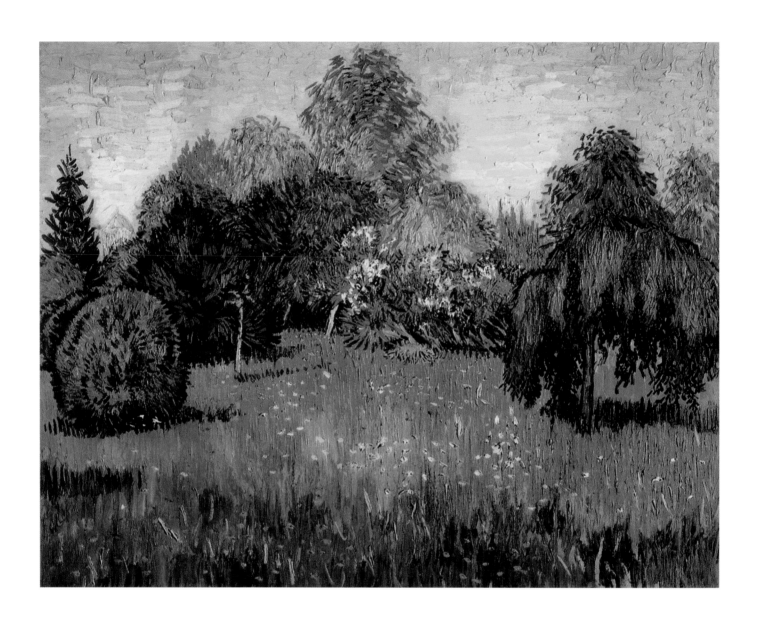

35. *The Poet's Garden*,
Arles, September
1888. Oil on canvas,
73 x 92 cm. Chicago,
The Art Institute of
Chicago.

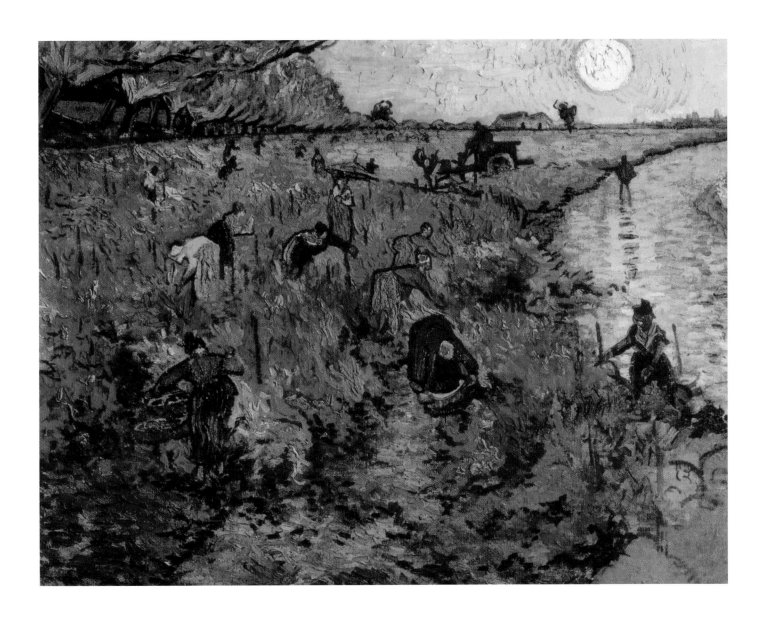

36. *The Red Vineyard*,
Arles, November
1888. Oil on canvas,
75 x 93 cm. Moscow,
Pouchkin Museum.

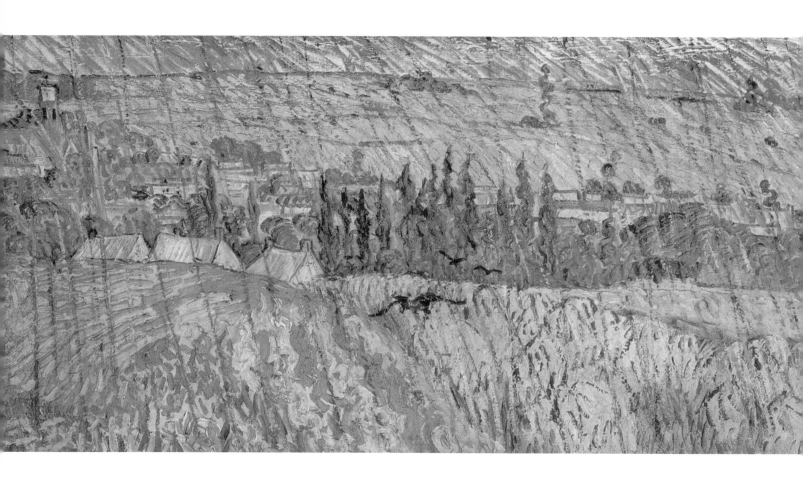

37. *Landscape of Auvers in the Rain*, Auvers-sur-Oise, July 1890, Oil on canvas, 50 x 100 cm, Cardiff, National Museum of Wales.

Tersteeg, Van Gogh's former master, sought to pressure him by asking Theo to stop the financial support. The painter was largely isolated in The Hague, and his relations with Sien became increasingly strained as money grew tight. During a visit, Theo convinced Vincent to abandon the relationship. At the end of 1883, Van Gogh joined his parents, who had moved to Etten, near Eindhoven. The return of the prodigal son was not a success. Because his family was unable to understand him – to know him – Van Gogh severed the connection. "They have the same dread of taking me in the house as they would about taking a big rough dog. He would run into the room with wet paws – and he is so rough. He will be in everybody's way. And he barks so loud. In short, he is a foul beast. [...] And I, admitting that I am a kind of dog, leave them alone." [29]

Van Gogh has often been criticized because of his appearance and his manners. He confesses that, in some periods of his life, he had neglected his clothes in order to ensure his solitude. He left the vicarage and rented rooms in the home of a Catholic

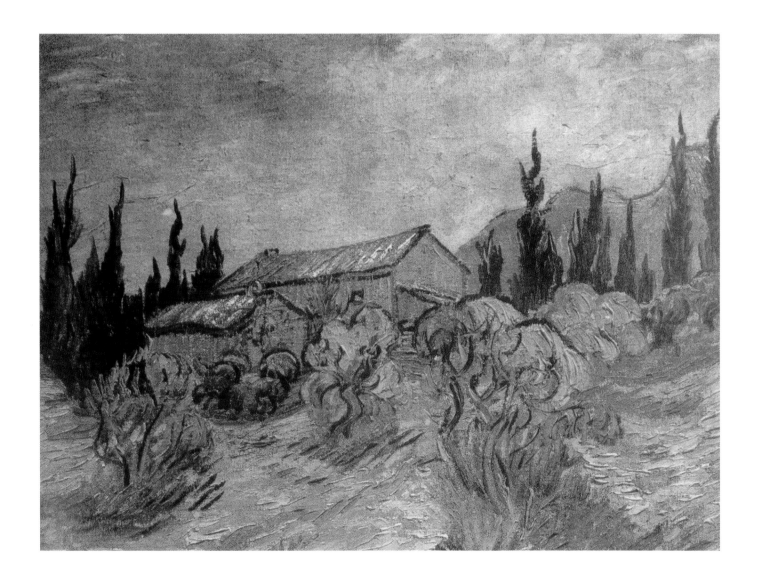

sexton. When he visited his father's house for a meal, he sat away from the family table: "I consciously choose the dog's path through life; I will remain the dog, I shall be poor, I shall be a painter, I want to remain human – going into nature." [30]

Van Gogh's artistic work in Nuenen is dominated by one central motif: the working man. The painter went into the fields and drew women digging out potatoes. He also sketched the weavers. In April 1885, he worked on the oil painting "The potato eaters," that today is considered to be his first masterpiece.

38. *Wooden Sheds*, Saint-Rémy, December 1889. Oil on canvas, 45.5 x 60 cm. Brussels, Private Collection.

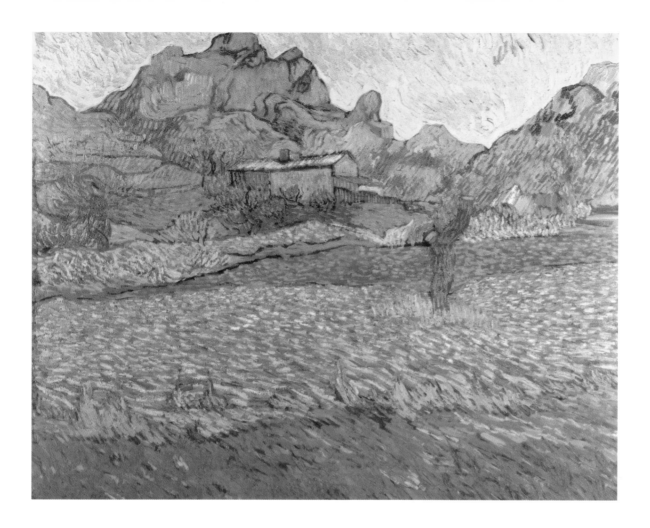

39. *A Meadow in the Mountains: Le Mas de Saint-Paul*, Saint-Rémy, mid-June 1889. Oil on canvas, 73 x 91.5 cm. Otterlo, Rijksmuseum Kröller-Müller.

40. *Cypresses with Two Female Figures*, Saint-Rémy, June 1889. Oil on canvas, 92 x 73 cm. Otterlo, Rijksmuseum Kröller-Müller.

He described the picture to Theo: "I have tried to emphasize that those people, eating their potatoes in the lamplight, have dug the earth with those very hands they put in the dish, and so it speaks of manual labor, and how honestly they earned their food. I wanted to give the impression of a way of life quite different from that of us civilized people. Therefore I am not at all anxious for everyone to like it or to admire it at once." [31] In November, 1885, he moved to Antwerp to join the Academy of Art. But he stayed there for only a short time. Four months later he left for Paris; he never returned to Holland.

He declared later that he hadn't become an adventurer by choice "but by fate, and feeling nowhere so much myself a stranger as in my family and country." [32]

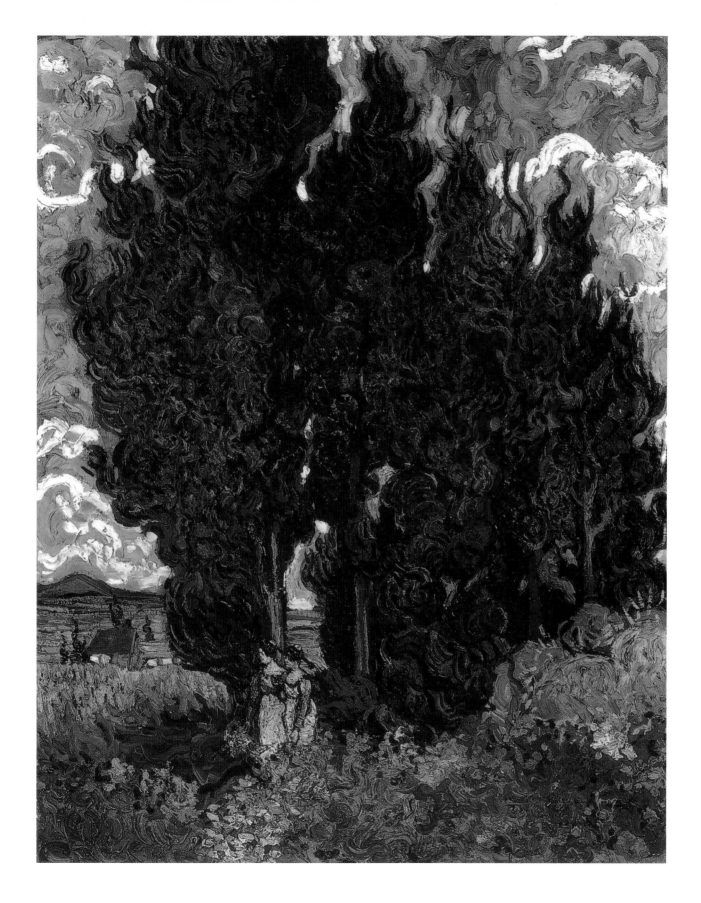

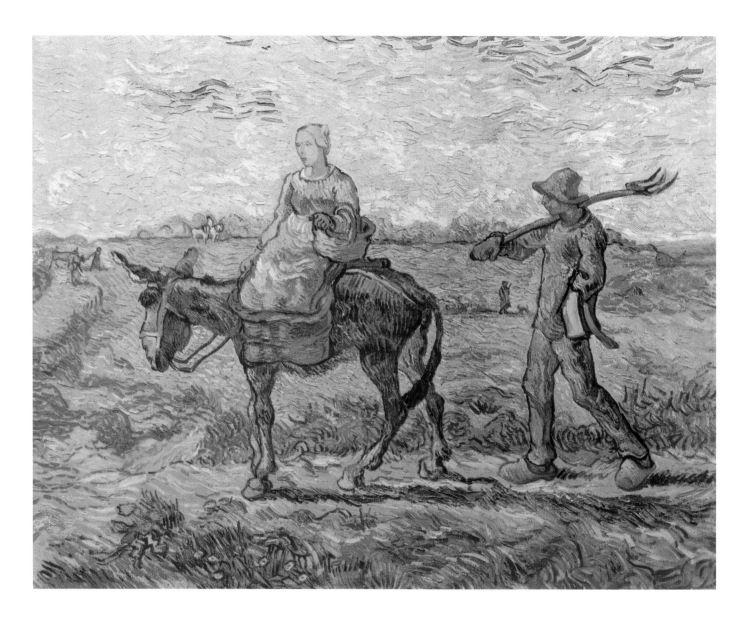

41. *Morning : Peasant Couple Going to Work* (after Millet), Saint-Rémy, January 1890. Oil on canvas, 73 x 92 cm. St. Petersburg, The Hermitage Museum

"The spreading of the ideas". Paris, 1886-1888

"And mind my dear fellow, Paris is Paris. There is but one Paris and however hard living may be here, and if it became worse and harder even – the French air clears up the brain and does you good – a world of good." [33] Van Gogh had been living in the French capital for nearly half a year when he wrote these euphoric sentences to Horace

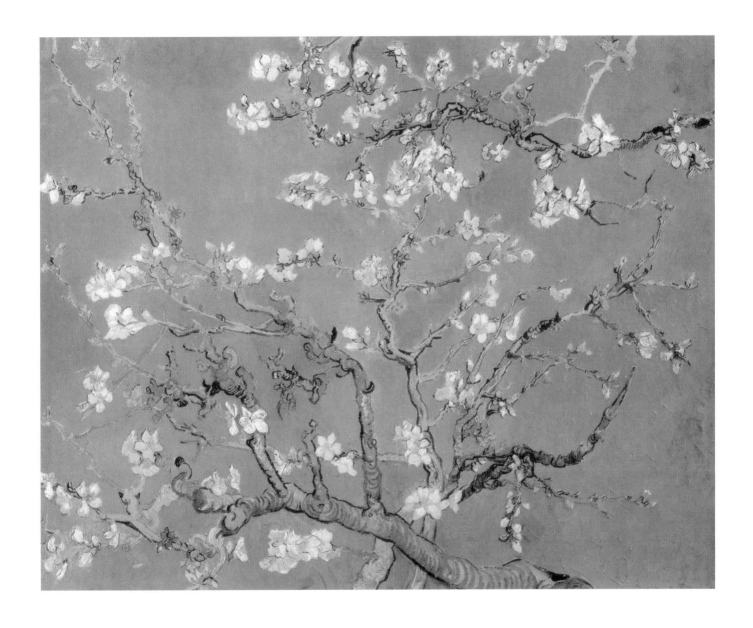

M. Levens, an English painter he had met in Antwerp. He had arrived unexpectedly in March, 1886. Van Gogh stayed in the capital of the 19th century for two years. Because he was living with his most significant correspondent, this chapter of his life is poorly documented. The cohabitation of the two brothers was not without its conflicts.

42. ***Blossoming Almond Tree***, Saint-Rémy, February 1890, Oil on canvas, 73.5 x 92 cm, Rijksmuseum Vincent van Gogh, Foundation Van Gogh, Amsterdam.

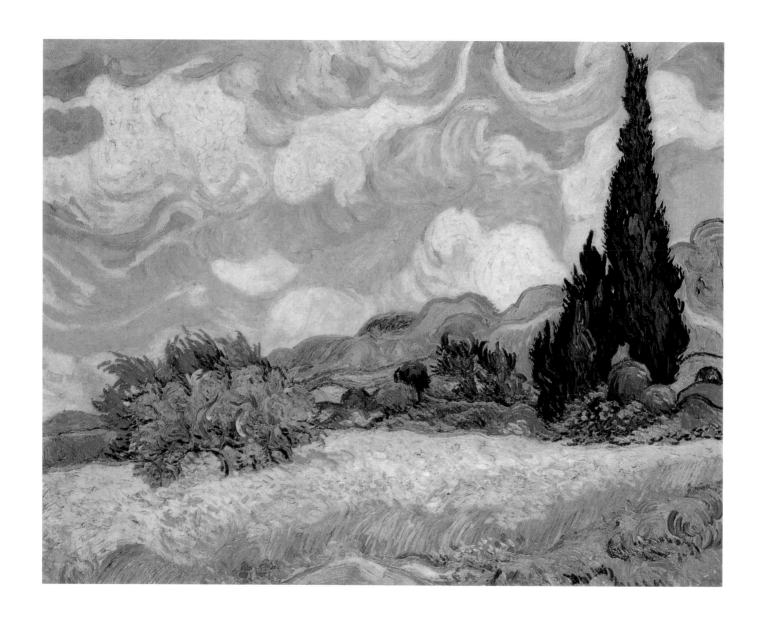

43. ***Green Wheat Field
with Cypress***, Saint-
Rémy, mid-June 1889.
Oil on canvas,
73.5 x 92.5 cm,
The Metropolitain
Museum, New York.

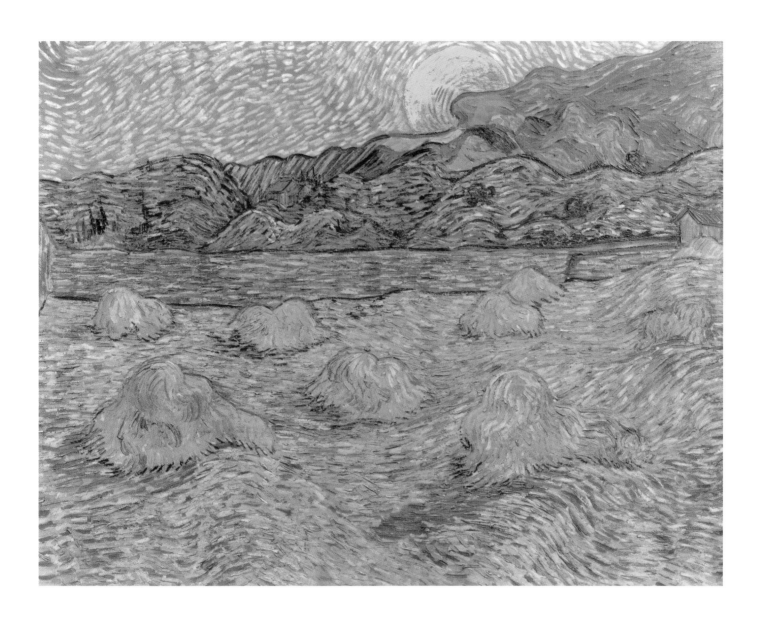

44. ***Evening Landscape
with Rising Moon***,
Saint-Rémy, Early
July 1889. Oil on can-
vas, 73 x 91.5 cm.
Otterlo, Rijksmuseum
Kröller-Müller.

The brothers eventually overcame this crisis, and drew closer than ever before. To Van Gogh, Paris offered a time for reflection and a time for painting. It was there that he first saw the Impressionist canvases of which Theo had written so often. He found work in the studio of Fernand Cormon, whose liberal way of teaching and disdain for the beaten track of the salons attracted many young painters. Henri de Toulouse-Lautrec and Emile Bernard also worked in Cormon's studio, and both befriended Van Gogh. Another student, François Gauzi, recalled that "When discussing 'art', if one disagreed with him and pushed him to the limit, he would flare up in a disturbing way. [...] He worked with a disorderly fury, throwing colours on the canvas with feverish speed. He gathered up the colour as though with a shovel, and the gobs of paint, covering the length of the paintbrush, stuck to his fingers. When the model rested, he didn't stop painting. The violence of his study surprised the atelier; the classically-oriented remained bewildered by it." [34]

Even more than the studio, the colour store of Julien Tanguy fascinated the young painter. Over his wife's protests, the proprietor occasionally let his customers pay for their supplies with paintings.

Tanguy's store thus became something of a gallery, where the painters met to see the work of their colleagues. It was here that Van Gogh came to know Paul Gauguin, whose paintings he greatly admired. The Scottish painter Archibald Standish Hartrick offers this impression of the conversations in Père Tanguy's store: Van Gogh "was particularly pleased with a theory that the eye carried a portion of the last sensation it had enjoyed into the next, so that something of both must be included in every picture made. The difficulty was to decide what were the proper sensations so coloured to combine together. The effects of colour also prompted Van Gogh's interest in the Japanese woodcuts he had first encountered in Antwerp. He had a sizable collection of these prints in Paris, and organized an exhibition of them in the café "Tambourin". The self-portrait was the main subject of Van Gogh's work from 1886 to 1888. In one canvas, he represents himself as a painter, with brush and palette. In the Paris that he once called a "spreading of ideas," [35] he found his way. In the summer of 1887, he wrote to his sister Willemien: "I have a dirty and hard profession – painting – and if I were not what I am, I should not paint; but being what I am, I often work with pleasure, and in the hazy distance I see the possibility of making pictures in which there will be some youth and freshness, even though my own youth is one of the things I have lost. [...] It is my intention as soon as possible to go temporarily to the South, where there is even more colour, even more sun. But the thing I hope to achieve is to paint a good portrait. But never mind." [36]

45. *Self-Portrait*, Saint-Rémy, late August 1889. Oil on canvas, 57 x 43.5 cm. New York, Private Collection.

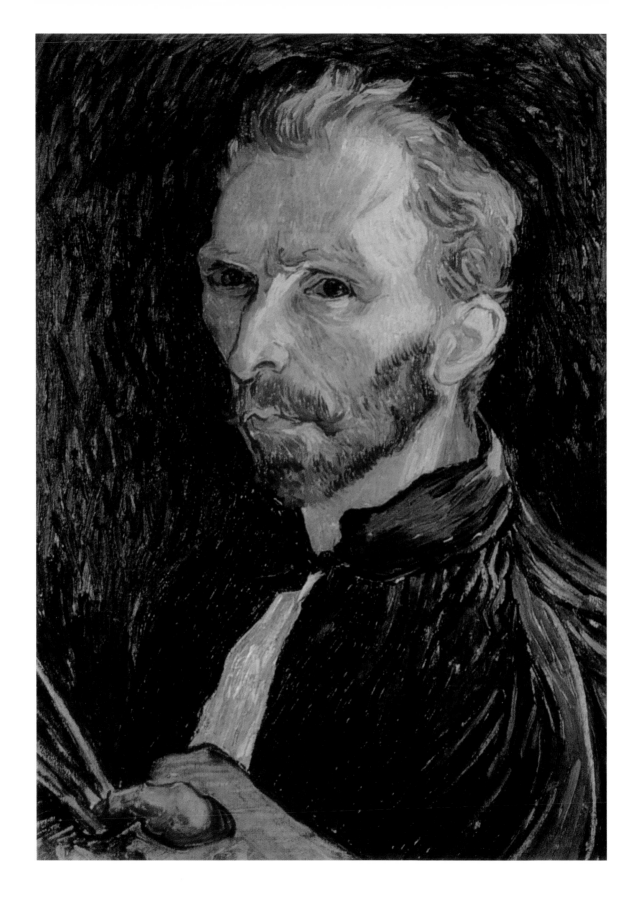

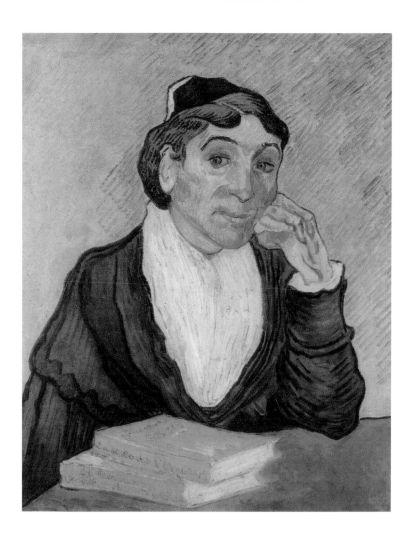

"An artists' house". Arles, 1888-1889

46. *L'Arlésienne*
    (*Madame Ginoux*),
    Saint-Rémy, February
    1890, Oil on canvas,
    65 x 54 cm, São
    Paulo, Museu de Arte
    de São Paulo.

47. *Self-Portrait*, Saint-
    Rémy, September
    1889, Oil on canvas,
    65 x 54 cm, Paris,
    Musée d'Orsay.

On February 19th, 1888 Van Gogh left Paris for Arles. He rented a room in the Carrel Inn and set to work immediately: In the morning, he went out into the fields and gardens, where he stayed until late afternoon. He spent his evenings in the Café de la Gare, where he wrote letters and read newspapers or novels like Pierre Loti's "Madame Chrysanthème." It was there that he befriended the Zouave second lieutenant Paul-Eugène Milliet, the postman Joseph Roulin, and the couple Ginoux, who owned the café. In May of the same year, he rented two rooms in an empty house on the Place Lamartine. Since the rooms were unfurnished, he slept in the Café de la Gare, having abandoned the Carrel Inn after a quarrel with the landlords. The task of decorating the house – which he called both the "Yellow House" and "the Artists' House" – delighted him to no end.

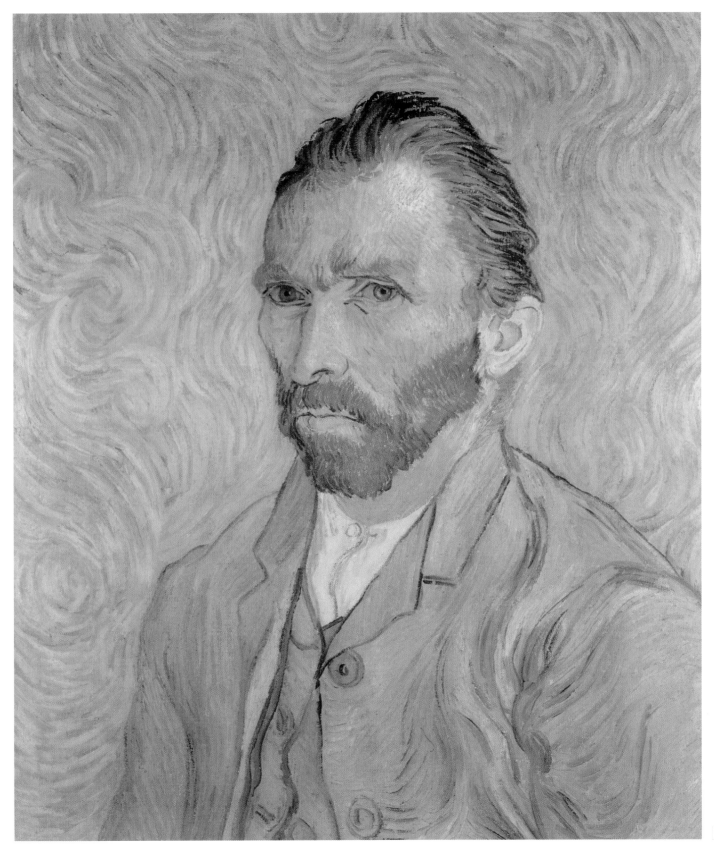

In his mind, it was to form the nucleus of an artists' colony, a studio of the South. "You know that I have always thought it idiotic the way painters live alone," he wrote to Theo. "You always lose by being isolated." [37]

Dependent on his family for financial support, Van Gogh began to reflect on the position of the artist in society: "All the same they are building State museums, and the like, for hundreds of thousands of guilders, but meanwhile the artists very often starve." [38] For Van Gogh, museums were cemeteries. He was similarly contemptuous of the art trade. Van Gogh's alternative to this unhappy state of affairs was a community of artists: The painters should work together, support each other and give their works to one, faithful dealer – Theo – who would pay a monthly sum to the artists, regardless of whether the works were sold or not.

Van Gogh tried to persuade Gauguin to join the studio of the South. For over half a year, from March to October 1888, he courted his admired colleague with letters. He asked Theo to increase his monthly allowance to 250 francs, so that Gauguin could live with him in Arles. In return, Theo would receive one painting from Gauguin.

Gauguin, who was living in Brittany, stalled in his replies: sometimes he claimed to be too ill to travel, and on other occasions to be short of funds.

The months of waiting for Gauguin were the most productive time in Van Gogh's life. He wanted to show his friend as many new pictures as possible. At the same time, he wanted to decorate the Yellow House. In the middle of August, he started the cycle of the sunflowers for the guest room. Of the projected twelve sunflower pictures, he completed only two, because the 'models' disappeared too quickly. He therefore turned to a new subject: the garden of the poet. Three variations on this theme, together with the two sunflower paintings became the decoration for the guest room, which was waiting for Gauguin's arrival.

On October 23rd, Paul Gauguin finally arrived in Arles. In the middle of November, Gauguin reported to his dealer and financial backer Theo: "The good Vincent and "le grièche Gauguin" continue to make a happy couple and eat at home the little meals they prepare themselves." [39]

Paul Gauguin saw himself in the position of a sage, and relegated Van Gogh to the role of his student: "Vincent, at the moment when I arrived in Arles, was fully immersed in the Neo-Impressionist school, and he was floundering considerably, which caused him to suffer; [...]. With all these yellows on violets, all this work in complementary colours – disordered work on his part – he only arrived at subdued, incomplete, and monotonous harmonies; the sound of the clarion was missing.

48. *Enclosed Wheat Field with Peasant*, Saint-Rémy, early October 1889, Oil on canvas, 73.5 x 92 cm, Indianapolis, Indianapolis Museum of Art

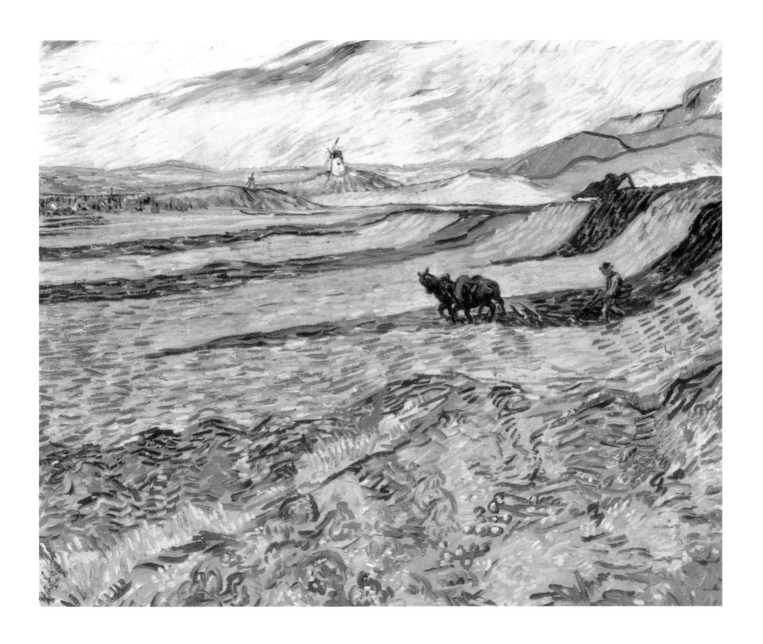

I undertook the task of enlightening him, which was easy for me, for I found a rich and fertile soil. Like all natures that are original and marked with the stamp of personality, Vincent had no fear of his neighbor and was not stubborn. From that day on, my Van Gogh made astonishing progress." [40]

Regarding the pictures Van Gogh painted before and after Gauguin undertook him, however, there is little evidence of this progress. In March, 1888 Van Gogh painted 'The Bridge at Langlois,' in July 'The Mousmé' and the 'Portrait of Joseph Roulin,' in August the 'Sunflowers,' in September 'The poet's garden,' 'The starry night,' 'The Yellow House,' the 'Self-portrait for my friend Paul Gauguin,' 'The café by night' and in October 'Vincent's room at Arles.' The very paintings that Gauguin dismissed as 'subdued, incomplete and monotonous' are today regarded as his greatest masterpieces.
With Gauguin at his side, Van Gogh painted less and without the force he had discovered earlier that year. Unlike Gauguin, Van Gogh needed reality as a model. He was not able to separate his thoughts from his subjects. He strove for a synthesis of reflection and the immediate feeling he had about the things and people he painted.

The love and hope he had introduced into his canvases while waiting for Gauguin were ultimately frustrated. Gauguin didn't share his views on art. That was painful enough, but Van Gogh was even more hurt by the way his friend disparaged him. He had already had a similar experience with Anton van Rappard, whom he had met in Brussels. Both artists exchanged letters during the years 1881 and 1885. In December, 1888, Gauguin wrote to Emile Bernard: "In general, Vincent and I rarely agree on anything, especially on painting. He admires Daumier, Daubigny, Ziem, and the great Rousseau, none of whom I can stand. And, on the other hand, he detests Ingres, Raphaël, Degas, all of whom I admire. [...] He loves my paintings, but when I'm doing them, he always finds that I've done this or that wrong. He is a romantic and I am more inclined to a primitive state. Regarding colour, he sees the possibilities of impasto as in Monticelli, whereas I hate the mess of execution, etc..." [41]

49. *View of the Church at Saint-Paul-de-Mausole*, Saint-Rémy, October 1889. Oil on canvas, 44.5 x 60 cm. United States, Collection Elizabeth Taylor.

At about the same time, Gauguin announced to Theo that he wanted to return to Paris: "Vincent and I absolutely cannot live side-by-side any longer without friction because of the incompatibility of our temperaments and because he and I both need tranquillity for our work." [42] Nobody knows, finally, what happened in the last days before Christmas. However, the bulk of the available information about the events of December 23rd, 1888 comes from a less than objective witness, Paul Gauguin: "Upon arriving at the square, I saw a large crowd assembled.

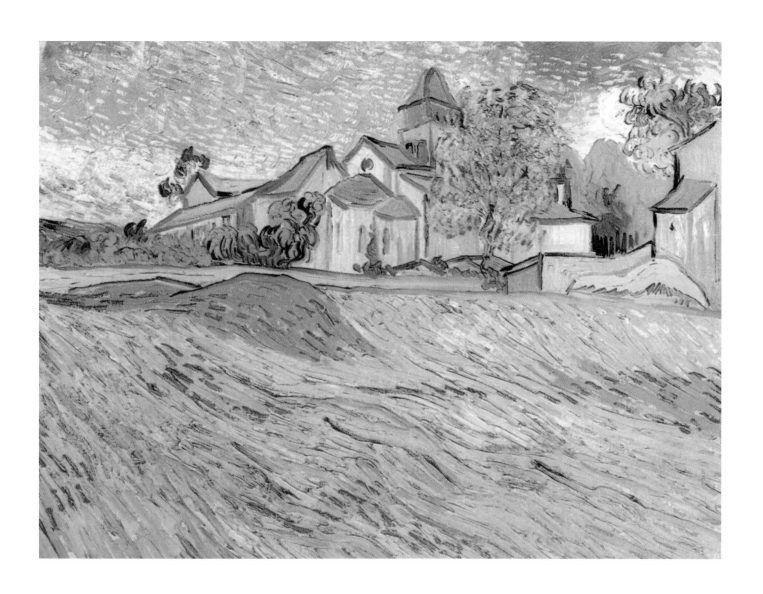

Near our house, there were some gendarmes and a little gentleman in a bowler hat, who was the police commissioner. Here is what had happened. Van Gogh returned to the house and, immediately, cut off his ear close to the head. He must have taken some time in stopping the heamorrhage, for the next day there were many wet towels scattered about on the floor tiles of two rooms downstairs. When he was in good enough condition to go out, his head covered up by a Basque beret pulled all the way down, he went straight to a house where, for want of a fellow-countrywoman, one can find a chance acquaintance, and gave the 'sentry' his ear, carefully washed and enclosed in an envelope. "Here," he said, "a remembrance of me." Then he fled and returned home, where he went to bed and slept. He took the trouble, however, to close the shutters and to set a lighted lamp on a table near the window. Ten minutes later, the whole street given over to the *filles de joie* was in commotion and chattering about the event. I had not the slightest inkling of all this when I appeared on the threshold of our house and the gentleman with the bowler hat said to me point-blank, in a more than severe tone: "What have you done, sir, to your comrade?" – "I don't know." – "Oh, yes, … you know very well, … he is dead." I would not wish anyone such a moment, and it took me a few long minutes to be able to think clearly and to repress the beating of my heart. Anger, indignation, and grief as well, and the shame of all those gazes that were tearing my entire being to pieces suffocated me, and I stuttered when I said, "Alright, sir, let us go upstairs, and we can explain ourselves up there." In the bed, Vincent lay completely enveloped in the sheets, curled up like a gun hammer; he appeared lifeless. Gently, very gently, I touched the body, whose warmth surely announced life. For me it was as if I had regained all my powers of thought and energy. Almost in a whisper, I said to the commissioner of police: "Be so kind, sir, as to awaken this man with great care and, if he asks for me, tell him that I have left for Paris. The sight of me could be fatal to him." [43]

Compared with the reports of other witnesses, such as that of the policeman Alphonse Robert, Gauguin's story is incorrect on some minor points. Van Gogh did not cut off his whole ear, but only a piece above the lobe. He gave this 'present' to the prostitute Rachel, and not to the 'sentry.'

Gauguin's account offers little insight into the motives behind his host's act of self-mutilation. Perhaps Van Gogh feared that his friend would make good his threat to leave him. Gauguin's departure would have been doubly traumatizing, for it also meant the end of the artists' house. Another reason for his distress might have been Theo's engagement with Johanna Bonger. Arnold tells us that Van Gogh was informed of his brother's plans to marry on December 23rd.

50. *Trees in the Garden of Saint-Paul Hospice*, Saint-Rémy, October 1889. Oil on canvas, 90.2 x 73.3 cm. Los Angeles, The Armand Hammer Museum of Art.

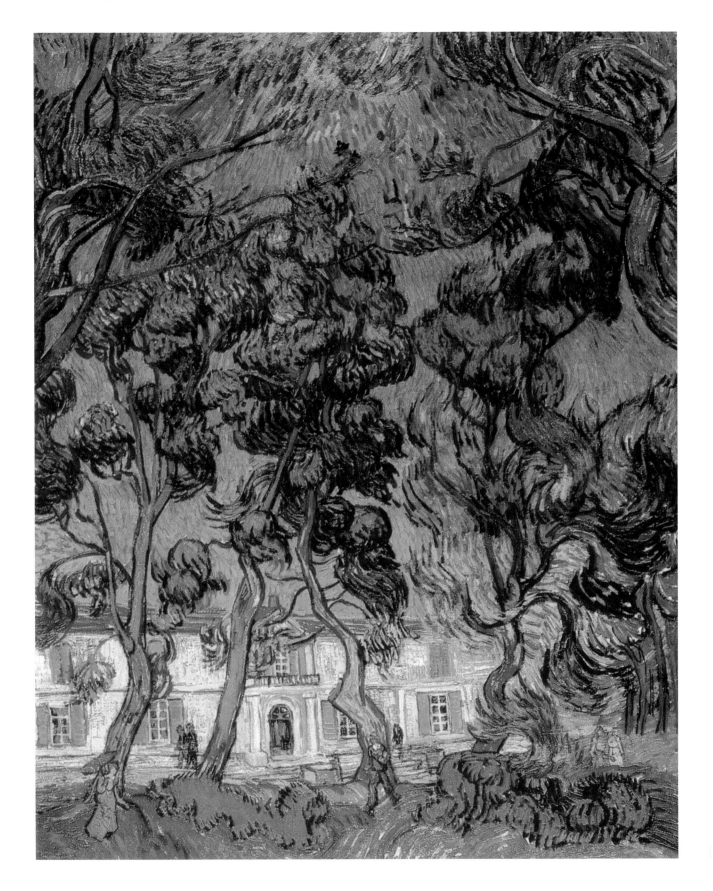

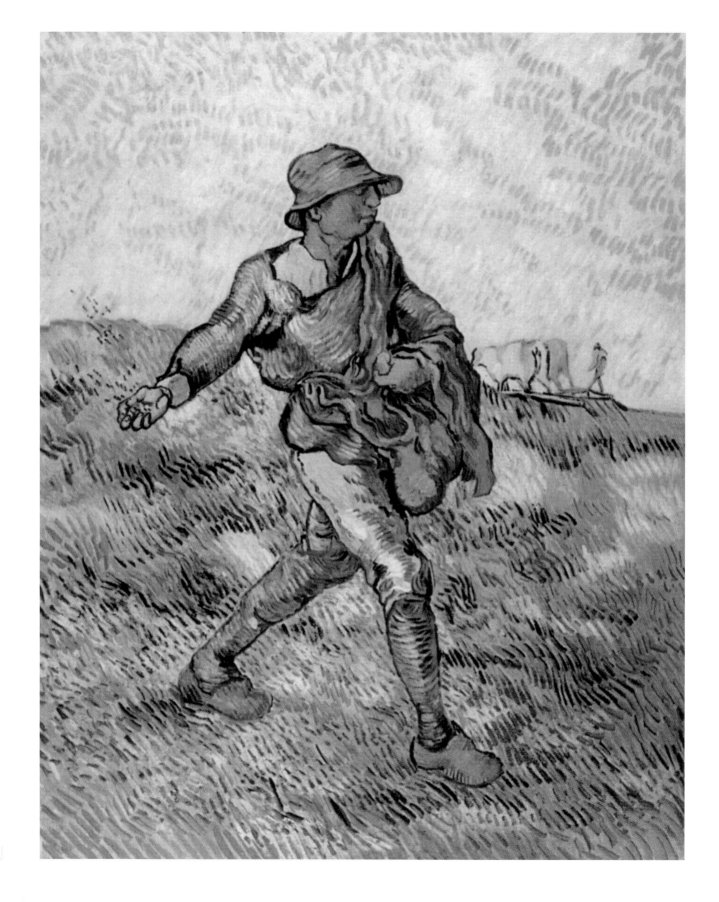

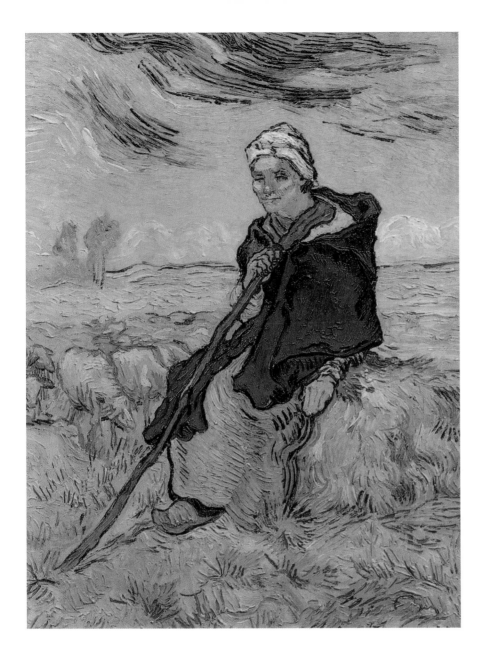

This change would surely have had an impact on his life. Perhaps Theo, faced with the expense of setting up his new household, would no longer be able to offer the support – financial or intellectual – on which his brother had come to depend.

Gauguin informed Theo about Vincent's crisis, and the younger Van Gogh arrived in Arles on December 25th, but stayed for only a very short time. In all likelihood, he returned to Paris the same day, accompanied by Gauguin.

51. *The Sower* (*after Millet*), Saint-Rémy, late October 1889. Oil on canvas, 80.8 x 66 cm. Collection Stavros S. Niarchos.

52. *The Sheperd* (*after Millet*), Saint-Rémy, November 1889. Oil on canvas, 52.7 x 40.7 cm. Tel Aviv, Tel Aviv Museum.

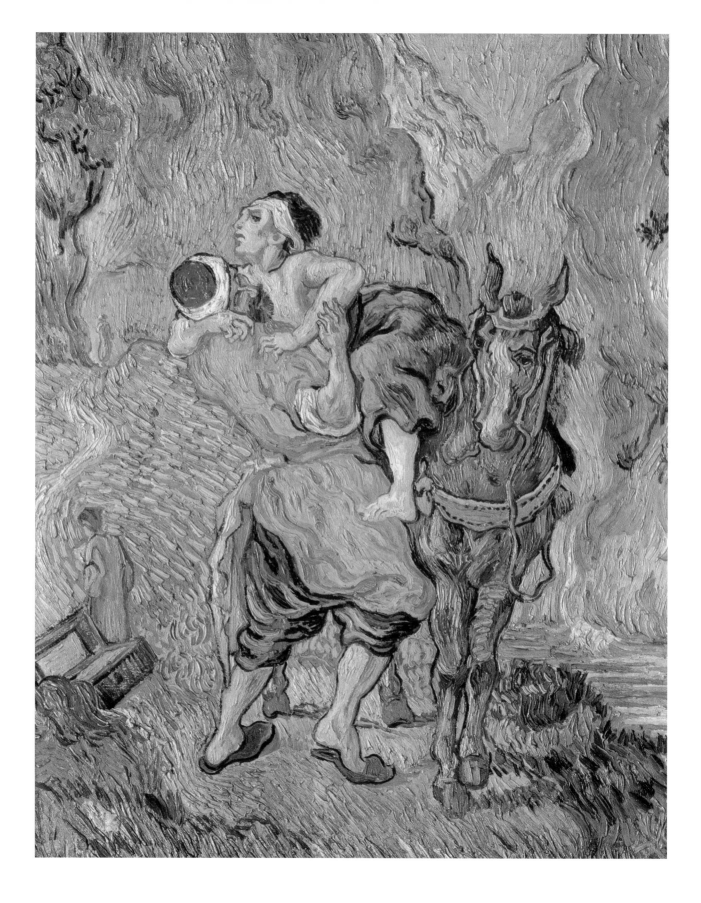

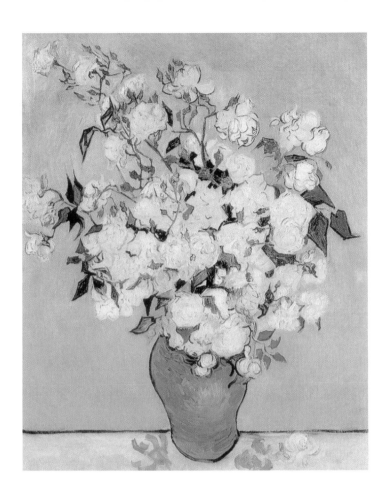

"I was a fool and everything I did was wrong". Arles, 1889

On January 7th, fourteen days after his self-mutilation, Van Gogh left the hospital. Joseph Roulin and his wife began to look after him. In the first letters after his return into the Yellow House, Van Gogh makes no mention of his madness.

Writing and painting, Van Gogh hoped to recover and to forget. He painted a portrait of his physician, Dr. Rey. Still, he clung to his belief in the future of the artists' house. During this period, Van Gogh worked on a painting he had already begun in December: a portrait of Augustine Roulin, the wife of the postman, that he calls 'La Berceuse.' The picture painted to comfort others became a consolation for himself. He wrote to Gauguin: "My dear friend, to achieve in painting what the music of Berlioz and Wagner has already done ... an art that offers consolation for the broken-hearted!" [44]

53. *The Good Samaritain* (*after Delacroix*), Saint-Rémy, May 1890. Oil on canvas, 73 x 60 cm. Otterlo, Rijksmuseum Kröller-Müller.

54. *Still-Life: Pink Roses in a Vase*, Saint-Rémy, May 1890. Oil on canvas, 92.6 x 73.7 cm. Rancho Mirage, California: Mr. And Mrs. Walter H. Annenberg Collection.

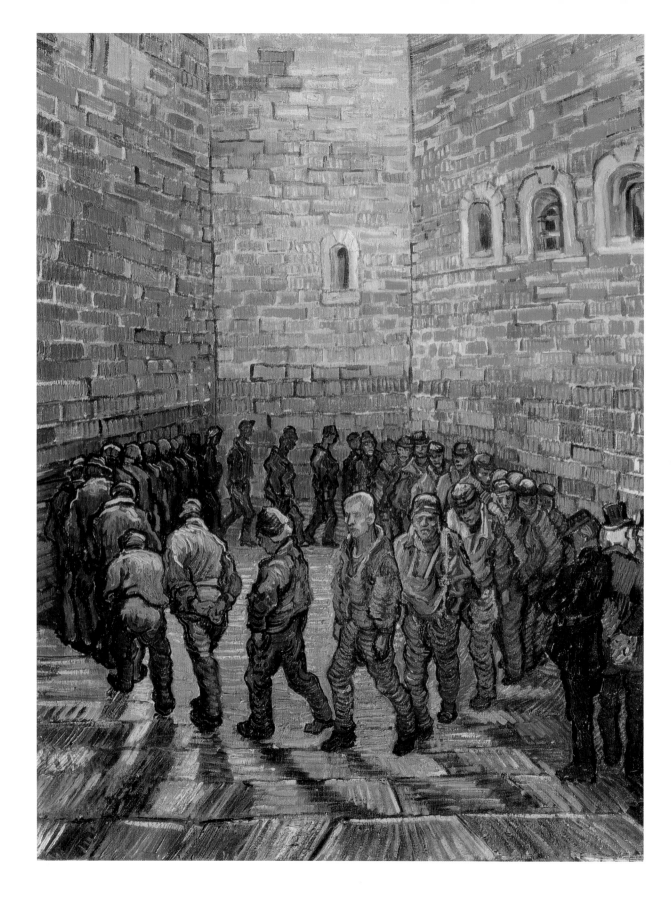

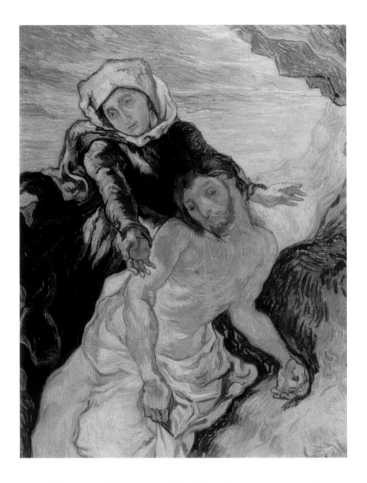

On February 7th, Reverend Salles, the Protestant clergyman, informed Theo: "Your brother [...] had again shown symptoms of mental derangement. For three days, he believes he sees everywhere people who poison and people who are poisoned. The charwoman [...] in view of his abnormal state, took it for her duty to report the affair; the neighbors informed the superintendent. He gave the order to watch your brother and admit him into the hospital [...] What shall be done now?" [45] Van Gogh saw himself as wrongly convicted, not ill. On several previous occasions he had learned that deviation from social conventions is often punished with exclusion. After Van Gogh's failure as a preacher, his father had threatened to admit him to the mental hospital in Gheel. [46] Tersteel, the manager of Goupil's gallery in The Hague considered him to be of "unsound mind and temperament" [47] when he learned that the painter was living with a prostitute. In his letters, Van Gogh uses madness and illness quite often as a metaphor for the state of society: "Then the doctors will tell us that not only Moses, Mahomet, Christ, Luther, Bunyan and others were mad, but Frans Hals, Rembrandt, Delacroix, too, and also all the dear narrow-minded old women like our mother.

55. *Prisoners' Round* (*after Gustave Doré*), Saint-Rémy, February 1890. Oil on canvas, 80 x 64 cm. Moscow: Pouchkin Museum.

56. *Pieta* (*after Delacroix*), Saint-Rémy, September 1889. Oil on canvas, 73 x 60.5 cm. Rijksmuseum Vincent Van Gogh, Foundation Van Gogh, Amsterdam.

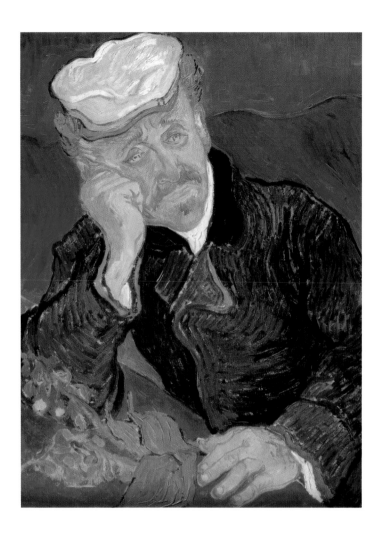

57. *Portrait of Doctor Paul Gachet*, Auvers-sur Oise, juin 1890. Oil on canvas, 68 x 57 cm. Paris, Musée d'Orsay.

58. *The Church at Auvers-sur-Oise*, June 1890. Oil on canvas, 94 x 74 cm. Paris, Musée d'Orsay.

Ah – that's a serious matter – one might ask these doctors: Where then are the sane people? Are they the brothel bouncers who are always right? Probably. Then what to choose? Fortunately there is no choice." [48] Van Gogh understood, from the beginning, the social side of his 'madness.' In time, he learned to accept that he was ill and that he needed help. But he didn't want to be punished: "If – say – I should become definitely insane – I certainly say that this is impossible – in any case I must be treated differently, and given fresh air, and my work, etc." [49] The mental hospital in Saint-Rémy, suggested by Pastor Salles, seemed to offer this treatment. Van Gogh also had other reasons to consent to going there: he had nowhere else to go. The owner of the Yellow House had cut off their contract; Gauguin refused to join him in Brittany; and his place in Theo's apartment was now occupied by the bride. He was afraid that he would again have to live in hotels: "I must have my own fixed niche." [50] The mental hospital became a shelter, a substitute for a home, a nest.

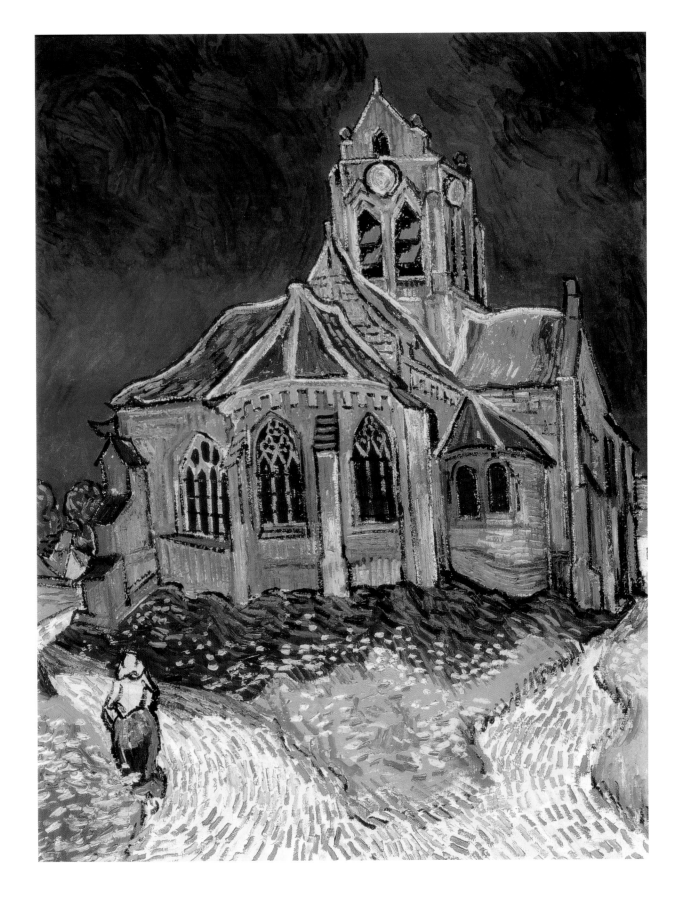

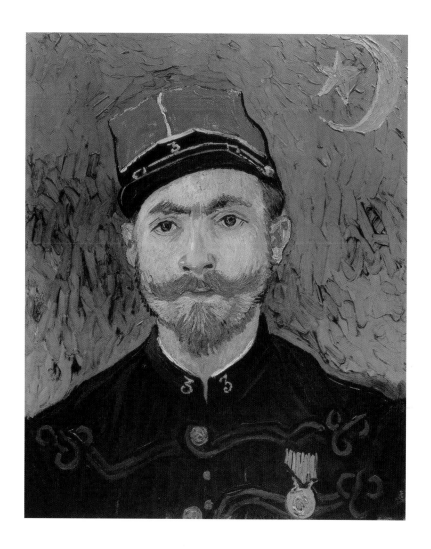

"What is the good of getting better?" Saint-Rémy, 1889-1890

59. *Portrait of Milliet*,
Sub-Lieutenant,
Zouave, Arles,
September 1888.
Oil on canvas,
81 x 65.5 cm. Otterlo,
Rijksmuseum Kröller-
Müller.

On May 8th, 1889 Pastor Salles took Van Gogh to the mental hospital in Saint-Rémy, thirty kilometers from Arles. The vague dread, or 'nameless fear' – an expression used by Van Gogh – disappeared as soon as the illness had a name. Van Gogh himself led Dr. Rey to believe that there was a history of epileptic attacks in his family. The doctor in Saint-Rémy accepted this diagnosis of his new patient without question. That the diagnosis was false finally did not matter very much: the treatment at Saint-Rémy was the same for all patients. They were bathed regularly; otherwise they were left on their own.

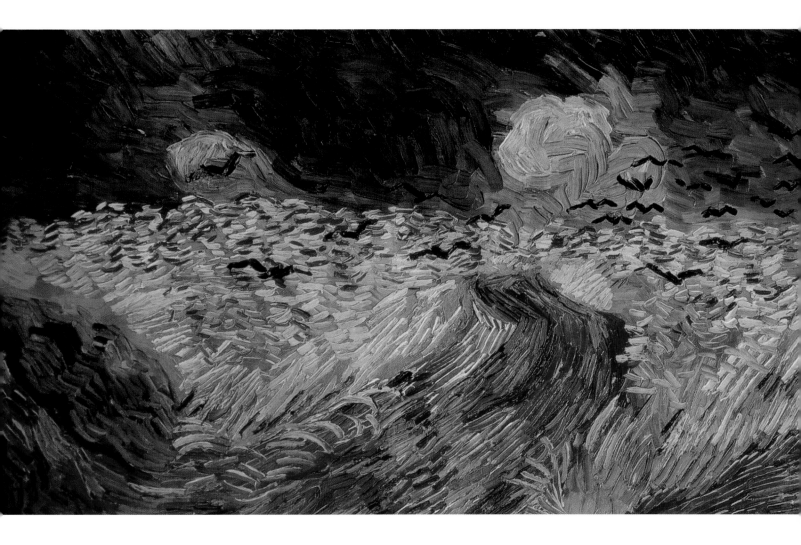

At the beginning, Van Gogh was impressed by the community of the sick, which seemed to him, in some parts, more human than the community of the healthy.

For the first time, Van Gogh felt that he was a part of the hospital community, but, in contrast with the other patients, he did not succumb to lethargy. Since he felt a duty to work, he started painting as soon as he arrived. He asked Theo to send him canvases and colours, along with a statement indicating how much he would have to produce in order to 'pay' for his stay.

During his stay in the hospital, Van Gogh painted landscapes, in which he recreated the world of his childhood anew.

60. ***Wheatfields with Crows***, June 1890. Oil on canvas, 50.5 x 105 cm. Rijksmuseum Vincent van Gogh, Foundation Van Gogh, Amsterdam.

At the same time, he continued to study the effects of colours: "The cypresses are always occupying my thoughts, I should like to make something of them like the canvases of the sunflowers, because it astonishes me that they have not yet been done as I see them. It is as beautiful of line and proportion as an Egyptian obelisk. And the green has a quality of such distinction. It is a splash of black in a sunny landscape, but it is one of the most interesting black notes, and the most difficult to hit off exactly what I can imagine. But then you must see them against the blue, in the blue rather. To paint nature here, as everywhere, you must be in it for a long time." [51]

Van Gogh again returned to his work, but his view of the hospital life had changed. The other patients, who had previously appeared to form an ideal community, now frightened him. Worse, the nuns who worked in Saint-Rémy terrified him. After the attack, Van Gogh would no longer leave the hospital to paint outdoors. It therefore became difficult for him to find subjects for his work. As an alternative he took himself as a model or copied one of the prints Theo had sent him from Paris. He 'repainted' the 'Pièta' by Delacroix and 'Prisoners' Round' by Gustave Doré.

"But there's nothing sad in this death…" Auvers-sur-Oise, 1890

Van Gogh stayed only three days with Theo and his family in Paris before leaving for Auvers-sur-Oise. The reason for his short stay may have been the quarrels between Theo and Johanna, which Van Gogh later described in his letters. Nature and work were, again, the twin supports in Van Gogh's life. But there were no people around him. Dr. Gachet proved to be of little help. Van Gogh: "I think we must not count on Dr. Gachet at all. First of all, he is sicker than I am, I think, or shall we say just as much, so that's that. Now when one blind man leads another blind man, don't they both fall into the ditch?" [52]

The 62 year old specialist in heart conditions and nervous diseases was a great art lover. He was in contact with many painters, and his collections, which were later given to the Musée d'Orsay in Paris, included paintings by Cézanne, Pissarro – and Van Gogh. The doctor was more interested in Van Gogh as a painter than as a patient.

Van Gogh lived in the Ravoux inn. Adeline, the daughter of the owner, at this time thirteen years old, sat for Van Gogh. So did the twenty-one-year-old Marguerite Gachet. A close friend of the doctor's daughter later claimed that the painter and his model had fallen in love, and Dr. Gachet forbade Van Gogh to come to his house any longer. Marguerite's brother confirmed the story in an interview, but changed it on one critical point: He said that his sister didn't return the affection of the 37-year-old painter.

61. *Plain at Auvers with Cloudy Skies*, Auvers-sur-Oise, July 1890. Oil on canvas, 73 x 92 cm. Otterlo, Rijksmuseum Kröller-Müller.

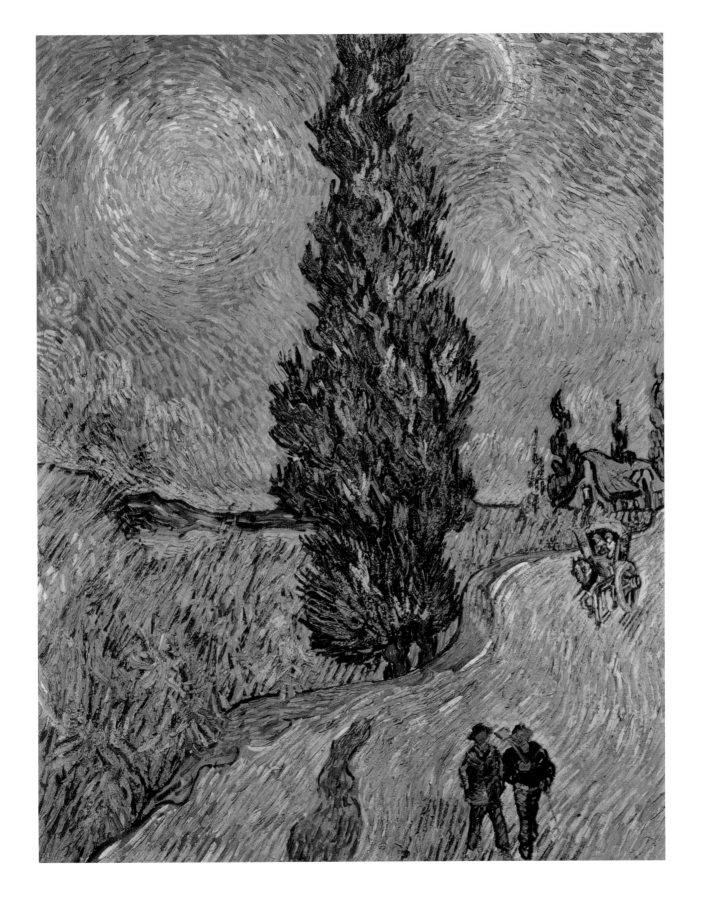

Obviously the friendship between Van Gogh and Gachet broke up soon; after July 2nd, Van Gogh stopped mentioning him in his letters.

During the two and a half months that he spent in Auvers, Van Gogh went through a cycle that he had already experienced several times. He tried to build up a regular life with work, but he lost sight of his security, of his nest. Increasingly, he felt that he was a burden for Theo. During a visit to Paris he was witness to a discussion between his brother and Johanna. Theo wanted to leave Goupil to found his own gallery; his wife preferred him to stay in the same position even though he didn't earn enough money. Vincent was not the only relative Theo had to support; he regularly sent money to his mother and his sister Willemien.

Ten years earlier, when Van Gogh started to depend on his brother's money, he wrote: "If I had to believe that I were troublesome to you or to other people at home, or were in your way, of no good for anyone, and if I should be obliged to feel like an intruder or an outcast, so that I were better off dead [...]. If it were indeed so, then I might wish that I had not much longer to live." [53] After his return from Paris Van Gogh described the canvases he was working on to Theo and Johanna: "They are vast fields of wheat under troubled skies, and I did not need to go out of my way to try to express sadness and extreme loneliness. I hope you will see them soon [...], since I almost think that these canvases will tell you what I cannot say in words, the health and restorative forces that I see in the country." [54]

This paradox – the sadness and health of the country – reflects Van Gogh's own situation: Nature always was a kind of home for him – a home that he could never share with anyone else.

In Saint-Rémy, Van Gogh had worked on a picture named 'The Reaper': "For I see in this reaper – a vague figure fighting like a devil in the midst of the heat to get to the end of his task – I see in him the image of death, in the sense that humanity might be the wheat he is reaping. So it is – if you like – the opposite of that sower I tried to do before. But there's nothing sad in this death, it goes its way in broad daylight with the sun flooding everything with a light of pure gold." [55]

62. *La Méridienne* (*after Millet*), Saint-Rémy, January 1890, Oil on canvas, 73 x 91 cm, Paris, Musée d'Orsay.

It is said that Van Gogh shot himself in a field, but there is little proof. If he had chosen the 'pure gold' of the wheat for his suicide, he decided, at least, not to die there lonely. After he had shot himself in his side, he returned to the inn and went to bed. The landlord informed Dr. Gachet and Theo. The brother described the last moments of Van Gogh's life which ended on July 29th, 1890: "I wanted to die. While I was sitting next to

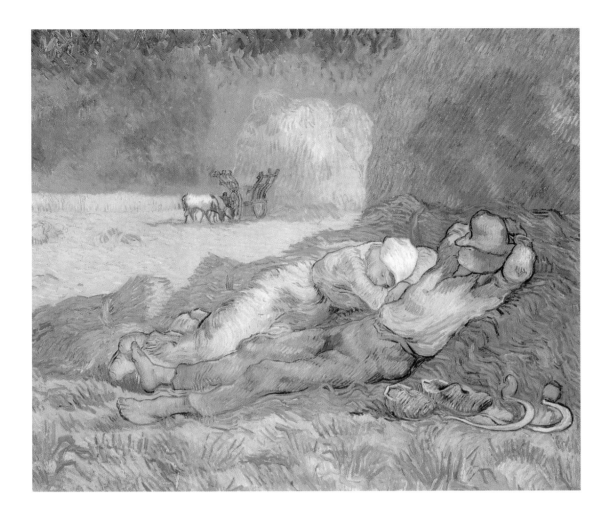

him promising that we would try to heal him [...],he answered: 'La tristesse durera toujours.' [The sadness will last forever.]" [56]

A few weeks before his suicide Van Gogh had written to Theo: "Even if I have not succeeded, all the same I think that what I have worked at will be carried on. Not directly, but one isn't alone in believing in things that are true. And what does it matter personally then! I feel so strongly that it is the same with people as it is with wheat, if you are not sown in the earth to germinate there, what does it matter? – In the end you are ground between the millstones to become bread. The difference between happiness and unhappiness! Both are necessary and useful, as well as death or disappearance... it is so relative – and life is the same." [57]

NOTES

1 Aurier, Albert: The isolated ones: Vincent van Gogh. In: Van Gogh. A retrospective. Edited by Susan Alyson Stein. New York 1988, p. 191.

2 Aurier, p. 191.

3 Aurier, p. 191.

4 Aurier, p. 191.

5 Arnold, Matthias: Vincent van Gogh. Biographie, München 1993, p. 1011.

6 L 164, in: The complete letters of Vincent van Gogh, Boston 19782, I: 285.

2. L 641a, in: The complete letters, III: 282.

3. Memoir of Vincent van Gogh by Johanna van Gogh-Bonger, in: The complete letters, I: XIX.

4. Van Gogh, Vincent: Sämtliche Briefe in sechs Bänden edited by Fritz Erpel: Berlin 1968, vol. 6: Dokumente und Zeugnisse, p. 93.

5. The complete letters, III: 594.

6. Huberta du Quense-Van Gogh: Vincent van Gogh (1910), in: Van Gogh. A retrospective, p. 32.

7. Van Gogh: Sämtliche, 5: 257.

8. L 573, in: The complete letters, III: 128.

9. L 418, in: The complete letters, II: 397.

10. L 133, in: The complete letters, I: 194.

11. L 332, in: The complete letters, II: 163.

12. L 20, in: The complete letters, I: 21 f.

13. L 94, in: The complete letters, I: 105.

14. L 85, in: The complete letters, I: 93.

15. The complete letters, III: 596 f.

16. see: Arnold: Vincent, p. 257.

17. L 131, in: The complete letters, I: 190.

18. L 133, in: The complete letters, I: 194.

19. L 133, in: The complete letters, I: 194.

20. L 159, in: The complete letters, I: 269.

21. L 212, in: The complete letters, I: 396.

22. L 197, in: The complete letters, I: 366.

23. R 8, in: The complete letters, III: 323.

24. L 117, in: The complete letters, I: 159 f.

25. L 182, in: The complete letters, I: 328.

26. L 346, in: The complete letters, I: 321.

27. L 347, in: The complete letters, II: 234.

28. L 404, in: The complete letters, II: 370.

29. L 459 a, in: The complete letters, II: 515.

30. L 459 a, in: The complete letters, II: 515.

31. François Gauzi: Lautrec et son temps (1954), in: Van Gogh. A retrospective, p. 71 f.

32. A. S. Hartrick: A painter's pilgrimage through fifty years (1939), Van Gogh. A retrospective, p. 82.

33. W 1, in: The complete letters, III: 435.

34. W 1, in: The complete letters, III: 425 ff.

35. L 463, in: The complete letters, II: 525.

36. L 493, in: The complete letters, II: 577.

37. L 438, in: The complete letters, II: 454.

38. Paul Gauguin: Avant et après (1903), in: Van Gogh.

39. A retrospective, p. 128.

40. Gauguin: Avant, p. 125.

41. Van Gogh. A retrospective, p. 130.

42. Van Gogh. A retrospective, p. 130.

43. Gauguin: Avant, p. 125 ff.

44. The letters of Vincent van Gogh, selected and edited by Ronald de Leeuw, translated by Arnold Pomerans, London 1996, p. 430.

45. Arnold: Vincent, p. 751.

46. Arnold: Vincent, p. 257.

47. L 216, in: The complete letters, I: 407.

48. L 516, in: The complete letters, III: 3.

49. L 579, in: The complete letters, III: 140.

50. L 579, in: The complete letters, III: 140.

51. L 596, in: The complete letters, III: 185.

52. L 648, in: The complete letters, III: 294.

53. L 132, in: The complete letters, I: 193.

54. L 649, in: The complete letters, III: 295.

55. L 604, in: The complete letters, III: 202.

56. Sämtliche Briefe, 6: 52.

57. L 607, in: The complete letters, III: 218.

63. *The Old Sad Man*, Saint-Rémy, April-May 1890. Oil on canvas, 81 x 65 cm. Otterlo, Rijksmuseum Kröller-Müller.

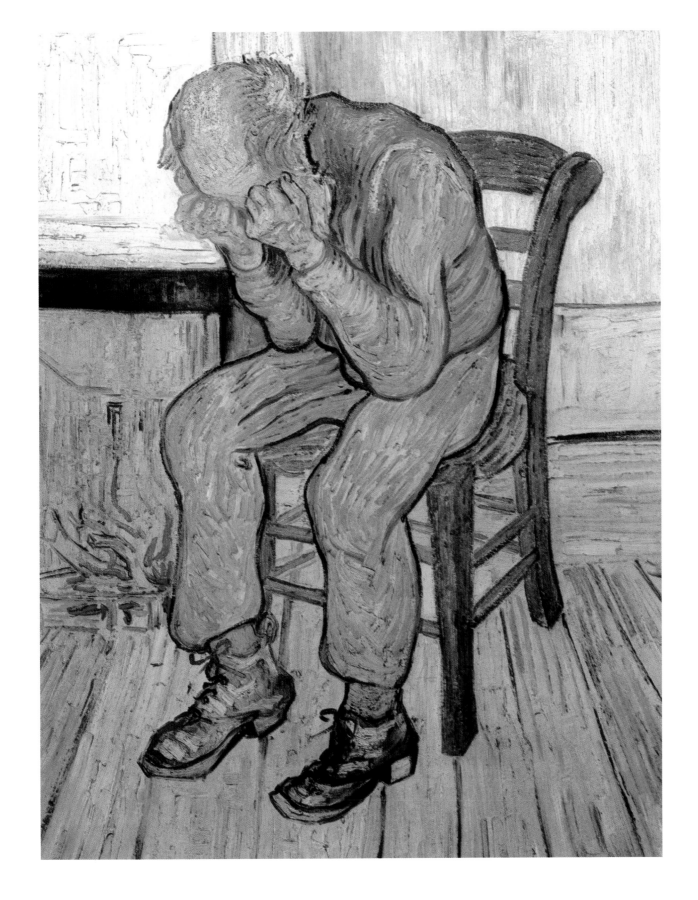

LIST OF ILLUSTRATIONS